CAPITAOL

BUYING OUR DEMOCRACY
WITH STOLEN MONEY

HARRY BROKASS

This is a work of fiction. Names, characters, business, places, events and incidents are either the products of the author's imagination or used in a fictitious manner. Any resemblances to actual persons, living or dead, or actual events are purely coincidental.

ISBN: 0615550096
ISBN 13: 9780615550091
LCCN: 2011918310
Eric Thomas, Orlando, FL

9 DAYS

Preface: Discovering the World's Finest Highly Addictive Vodka Is My Secret to World Domination Right after I Become the President of The United States with Stolen Money from Rigged Capitalism by Goldballs'n Sak

It all started with vodka. Vodka—or rather, my obsession with perfecting the world's finest variety of it—started a chain of events that changed everything. This vodka motivated me to buy the presidency of the United States with stolen money. It was the beginning of profiting on the collapse of our global financial system into what will rightfully be called the Great Depression II by the former middle class.

After working twenty-six years in Wall Street investment banking and establishing my own hedge fund, I retired a billionaire on July 7, 2007. This was the day of my thirty-year wedding anniversary. For five years my wife and I had split our lives between New York and our vineyard in Napa Valley, California. My wife grew up making wine in Italy and wanted to retire on our own vineyard by the beach. The love of my life began creating award-winning wines. It made me happy to enjoy starting a new life with her.

My name is Goldballs'n Sak. I am a vodka drinker. Being on Wall Street allowed me to travel the world experiencing the world's finest vodkas. To share our new life, my wife was going to make wine, while I would pursue my love of creating the world's finest vodka.

We expanded our testing lab to include vodka facilities. After six months of testing, I felt I had perfected the formula for the world's greatest vodka. It was smooth, highly filtrated, with a slight lime scent and taste. I immediately sent twelve cases to my Wall Street friends whom I trusted to verify its quality. They requested thirty-six cases more. Then they wanted two hundred cases. Finally they agreed that I had created the world's finest vodka. The vodka had one flaw—it was highly addictive.

Getting drunk making incredible vodka made me miss the power of my old life in New York. The vodka got me excited about getting involved in politics instead of just buying politicians. This time around, I wanted to go to Washington, DC by becoming the president of the United States in 2012. My supportive spouse agreed the challenge would be great for the both of us.

On a beautiful spring weekend with the vines and wild flowers in full bloom, my closest friends, Dick, Butch, and Chainsaw, visited me. Their private planes landed ten minutes from my home at four p.m. on Friday, February 8, 2008. They were to attend a $40,000 a plate political party fundraiser dinner at six p.m. the next day. Butch and Dick were going to spend the night, while Chainsaw had to stay in San Francisco for security reasons. All of us were planning on going golfing before we went to the dinner.

All three of them were influential elected officials. Dick Melong had been elected over twenty years ago, while Butch and Chainsaw had been in office eight years. Butch and Chainsaw are nicknames for the reputations they earned. Butch revolutionized legal stealing and got his nickname from the notorious robber Butch Cassidy. Chainsaw earned his reputation with a management style of torturing and destroying his opponents.

"I can't believe how beautiful your vineyard is," said Butch, after getting out of the armor-plated limousine with Chainsaw and Dick.

"Welcome! Great to see all of you had a safe trip," I said.

"Thanks for the invite. How about some vodka?" said Butch.

"Beautiful home," said Chainsaw.

"Everything is set up on the terrace. This way. It's a shame your wives could not come. My wife is in Italy visiting her mother," I told them.

"Great to get away from mine. I heard you have your own golf course," said Dick, shaking my hand.

"Yes, you can see it in the valley under the sunset," I replied as we strolled down the stone walkway. "Please have a seat at the bar. I have some fresh bread and crackers, and these are all local cheeses over here if you are hungry. My chef is available until seven if you want anything. What can I get you?"

"I heard you make the best cosmopolitans," said Butch.

"Yes, I use all freshly squeezed ingredients. I use pomegranate instead of cranberry juice," I said.

"I have to try it," said Butch.

"Me too," said Dick.

"Same here after that long trip," said Chainsaw.

"Give me a second to get this ready," I said. I used two juicers to quickly prepare the drinks. "Here you go." Everybody showed their approval.

"This is an impressive home," said Chainsaw.

"Thanks. It is good to see all of you dressed casually because it has been in the eighties with no rain expected this weekend," I said.

"Great! I'm over the cold this year," said Chainsaw.

"My wife just redecorated this terrace. The old furniture was hurting my back. She wanted modern furniture with the old stonework. Let's move to the patio to watch the incredible sunset," I said. "We have a lot to celebrate. You will be leaving office and starting a new life."

"It's about time," said Butch. He grabbed the vodka bottle and shot glasses from the bar. "Excellent! Let's do shots," he said while pouring.

"Cheers," said all.

I said, "You will think I am crazy when you hear my next adventure. I am going to run for president of the United States in 2012."

"Wow! I didn't see that coming," said Dick.

"You can have it. I'm out of there," said Butch.

"If Butch can get elected, then anybody can," said Chainsaw, laughing.

"I see you already gave up on 2008!" said Dick, smiling.

"Let's have another round," said Butch.

"Here's a pitcher of cosmopolitans. Help yourself," I said while topping everybody off.

"I guess all of us can agree that OBaby Domay will become president, no matter what our party does," said Dick.

"We are going to profit off the Great Depression II," said Butch.

"You got that right," said Chainsaw. "How could we screw our country any more?"

"We are doing great, and that is what matters. I can win the 2012 election," I said.

"I cannot believe we will put up with OBaby as president," said Dick. "I refuse to do anything that would help him."

"Don't worry. Americans are so screwed. We destroyed generations. Nothing will improve for years," said Butch.

"You got that right. Also, nobody can complain because they got what they voted for," said Chainsaw, laughing.

"Is the rumor true about OBaby having a blue unicorn stuffed animal wherever he goes?" I asked.

"I actually looked into this. It is true," said Butch smiling. "Some Swedish cheerleaders he met in his sexual addiction program gave it to him when he was in college. It gave him hope throughout his career. He thinks it is magical, and it must go everywhere he goes."

"If he gets elected, we have to steal it," I said.

"We can plan that," said Butch.

"Now, I want to steal the money to finance my campaign," I said. "Our financial system is going to collapse when we decide. All of us have in some way contributed to creating Wall Street enigmas that are too enormous and convoluted to regulate. These 'too big to fail' companies will bring down the global financial system. We have to adapt, and entities survive by profiting from this destruction. We need to profit from destroying our clients, shareholders, and taxpayers. We need to plan when to destroy the financial system so we can all short the market to make money when investments decline in value. People are starting to figure out that Wall Street has been selling and insuring worthless securities because homeowners are beginning to default."

"Everything has been done legally. None of us will go to jail," said Chainsaw.

"I can assure you that our government will continue to tell the lie that everything is fine with our economy," said Dick.

"Wait! I need to start the fire pit. My wife will shoot me if I don't," I said while switching on the gas fire in the red stone pit.

"Let's have more shots," said Butch, pouring my best blue agave tequila as we all sat around the fire pit.

"I need this," said Chainsaw.

"Cheers," said everyone.

"What month do we want to do this?" I asked. "My vodka production will be at full capacity in October of this year. We will need it to successfully destroy our economy."

"It has to be before this year's election. I vote for October, too," said Dick.

"I have family commitments in November and December. October gets my vote," said Butch.

"October will work. This will give us a few months to keep the scam going," said Chainsaw.

"I can work with October. We will make billions off this," I said. "I will use everything I can steal to buy the presidency. This cannot happen without all your help."

"Planning for dealing with a collapsed financial system will be tricky. You will need government assistance to survive. The US Congress will have its pants down and be willing to do anything. No regulations have been in our way, and this won't change," Dick said.

"It is time start buying gold," Butch said, and broke out into a big belly laugh. "My planning is done."

"We can coerce politicians into giving us the entire farm for Christmas," I said.

"As long as we get tax cuts, we can have the entire farm for free, along with a golf course!" Dick said.

"No matter what happens, we win," said Chainsaw.

"I agree. My eight years are up. Its time to cash in," said Butch.

"I retired because of my concern that our financial system would collapse from fraudulent mortgages and worthless securities and that they were going to destroy us. I took the money and ran to my home here," I said.

"As a senior member of Congress, let me assure you that we will continue to cover your calculated and fixed betting. What is good for Wall Street is good for Congress. Congress is watching your back," said Dick.

"How can our government justify bailing us out if we make sure they guaranteed the fraud mortgages that are defaulting now?" I asked. "Our government is going to go broke paying for deceptive business practices. I understand that we own Congress, but at some point people will realize that they are paying our losses. We make billions on mortgage fraud and can cash in again when the financial system implodes. We rigged the system."

Butch emphatically said, "The mindless voter sheep have been scammed with fraudulent mortgages on a real estate bubble that I created to get re-elected. The system is rigged so let them pick up the tab. For you to get elected, real estate will need to stay depressed. All of us must make sure that nobody who owns a home gets help."

Chainsaw said, "I agree. The American dream of home ownership must end if you want to be president in 2012. Only Wall Street needs to be helped."

"Without growth in real estate and related businesses, jobs will be destroyed. Our economy will stay depressed," I said. "Because real estate depends on debt, credit must end."

"We can double down on the Great Depression II by leaving homeowners with only bankruptcy and foreclosure as options. This will kill their credit and hurt real estate and our economy even more," said Dick.

"The wealth of the American people has already started to decline. They must be ignored for us to receive government assistance and for me to get elected. I will have enough vodka to handle anything," I replied with a laugh. "Let's have another round. Does anybody want a cigar because these are my best?" I asked as everybody cut and lit them.

"This is excellent," said Dick.

"Are you dying your hair now?" Butch asked Dick.

"Yes, I need to get elected," said Dick smiling.

"We are all old and grey," said Chainsaw.

"I am trying to stay in office. You and Butch are now looking for work after your term," said Dick.

"Yes. Any ideas?" said Chainsaw.

"I will go wherever Chainsaw goes," said Butch, pouring a shot.

"Is everybody OK with another round?" I asked. Everybody showed approval. I went to the bar and made another pitcher of cosmos and wheeled it out with plenty of ice. "Here are freshly chilled glasses," I said while pouring another round.

"I have plenty of insurance extortion industry contacts. The both of you are perfect for this business," said Dick to Butch and Chainsaw.

"We need to cash in," said Butch.

"I am done working for free," said Chainsaw.

"Good," said Dick.

"Let's make sure we all have the same understanding," I said to the group. "Banks fraudulently loaned Americans money to buy their dream home. We're going to slap them in the face by having the government give us a bailout while they struggle to pay their mortgage. This is going to be fun!"

"Wait, it gets even better," Chainsaw exclaimed. "The worthless securities on those fraudulent mortgages were insured. Our government is going to pay the insurance claims as they default on paying. This is a double win for us."

"Somebody has planned this as if they knew every move we would make. The deal is designed so well that even if we screw up, we win. Once Americans realize what Wall Street has done, they will be screwed and broke. Our government will be left with the bar tab," said Dick.

"It's not just the bar tab. Our government is going to pay for Wall Street's $10,000-an-hour whores and drugs too," I said.

"I have to say this is the best vodka I have ever had," Butch said, yawning.

"Let's do another round!" I said and topped off everybody's glass.

"Let's make sure we steal as much as possible," Butch said. "Nobody will be able to stop us."

"After the quick October oh-eight flash crash, investors will not have time to react. We can make money on the way down, but also on the way up. The market will be suffering post-traumatic stress syndrome. At this time we can place our bets to make money on the way up. Nobody will be in our way," I said.

"This is why we need you back," said Butch.

"Yes," said Chainsaw, trying to stay awake.

"As usual, we have to make the stealing legal," Dick said, his words starting to slur a little. "To protect businesses, we're drafting up new legislation. Wall Street will always own our government, so we need to take action now to protect our interests. It is called the Dick Melong Wall Street Reform and Rewarding

Extortion Act. I'm too drunk to cover what all is in it."

"We have other issues besides flash crash conspiracy planning," I said.

A security agent went up to Chainsaw to remind him it was time to leave. "Gosh, this will take time to sink in. It's 8:05, bedtime for me, and I need to get into town," said Chainsaw.

"See you tomorrow," I said. Chainsaw gave his good night and left.

"My briefings will need to be done later because I am too drunk," said Butch.

"I never really believed you were going to retire, but nothing prepared me for this," said Dick to me.

"Let's discuss this more tomorrow," I said. "We can golf anytime tomorrow on my golf course. I even have a putting green and driving range. There are lights everywhere because I sometimes do night golfing."

I got up and began to walk inside with everybody. "I hope you find your rooms satisfactory. There's a shower with twenty showerheads in each bathroom, along with jet tubs. There is a full bar in the bathroom. My staff has put a menu by the phone at the bar if you get hungry. Your rooms are down the hall here.

"My chef can make breakfast anytime," I continued. "There is no schedule here. Great to see all of you."

"Good night," said Dick as everybody walked inside.

"I'm ready for golfing," Butch said, laughing.

It was a cool, quiet night with the windows open.

Chainsaw arrived back around eight a.m. and came out to the terrace, where I was at the bar filling my largest cooler with beer. He sat down at a barstool in the shade.

I said, "I'm icing down the beer if you're up for golfing."

"Definitely, even though my swing sucks," said Chainsaw, smiling.

Butch came out to the bar and said, "Ha, ya'll! Can I help with anything?"

"Can you please open the champagne bottle? I'm going to make mimosas with fresh orange juice," I said, plugging in the juicer and cutting the oranges.

"I smell cinnamon," said Chainsaw.

"My cinnamon rolls are ready," I said and opened the oven. "They just need to glaze."

"Good morning! Wow, fresh air! Mimosas," said Dick. He grabbed a champagne glass and poured out of the pitcher. "Have I missed anything?"

"Goldballs'n Sak is doing all the work. I'm waiting for my cinnamon roll. Chop! Chop!" said Chainsaw, laughing.

"Ready!" I said, offering cinnamon rolls to everyone. They devoured them.

"Lets not talk shop on the course," said Dick, pouring another mimosa.

"Fine with me," said Chainsaw.

"OK," said Butch.

Dick said, "We have to discuss the opening of Super Congress World in December 2008. Our entire careers have been involved in either planning or building the facility. You, Butch and Chainsaw, built it over the past eight years, while Goldballs'n Sak and I spent five years planning it. Everything has been built below the Capitol Visitor Center and Congress as planned. Nobody will ever figure out that it took eight years to build because we built another world underneath Congress."

"Finally! I can't believe it has been eight years of construction already. Nobody will believe we built a new Congress. This will protect our wealth for generations," said Butch.

"Stolen money will finance my presidency," I said.

"This will be our greatest accomplishment for our country. We rebuilt it to do everything we want. Let's toast to Super Congress World!" said Chainsaw.

"Cheers!" everybody said, touching glasses.

"The secret underground floors, especially level seven, are causing major technical problems. It will cost an additional seven hundred million dollars for the extra technological improvements and gold fixtures. I cannot believe we've been working on this since 2000. Wall Street has already spent forty billion dollars on the secret floors," said Dick.

"The money is no object; I'm stealing it, anyway," I said. "Please continue to make sure there is no transparency or accountability. I will need Super Congress World to become president. Also, the secret underground complex will help us rebuild with corporate welfare after the October 2008 crash."

"Super Congress World will allow us to steal whatever we want and stay out of jail," said Dick.

"When I become president, we will be in the free and clear no matter what," I said. "Let's decide what we want for breakfast. You will love my chef. Here are today's selections," I said, handing everybody a menu. "These are just suggestions. She can make whatever you want."

All of us got trashed having an incredible breakfast when Dick declared, "I'm ripped! Lets go golfing."

Day 1: Twelve-Step Credit Addiction Program; or, Let's Spin The Loaded Dice Again by Harry Brokass

When I look back on getting my presidential campaign going, nine days in January of 2012 started the chain of events that would forever change politics. It was Thursday, January 5, 2012, Dick Melong would not be able to host my Wall Street Annual Corporate Welfare Extortion Awards Luncheon because of a scheduling conflict. I made one of the biggest mistakes of my life by e-mailing Harry Brokass to ask him if he could host the event. He e-mailed back quickly at 9:20 a.m. that he would be there.

Harry Brokass was elected on a platform of reforming Congress from corruption and abuse of power. He had been a certified public accountant for over twenty years and felt a desire for public service. Harry used the equity in is home in Florida to finance his campaign. His home had decreased in value by 60 percent since he bought it in 2005. Struggling to pay bills had become too much of an ordeal. Winning his election was the beginning of improving his life. He never anticipated how much time he would have off.

After being on Christmas vacation for five weeks with full pay and benefits, Harry was required to attend credit counseling to meet the requirements of the Han Jahb Loan Modification and Credit Addiction Program at Steptin Schibt Bank, which allows borrowers to modify their home mortgages. This was important legislation for the middle class recovery; it requires borrowers to attend credit counseling. He refused to use any of his political status to influence the process.

Wise Abe was a broke credit counselor. Abe's current paycheck was less than it was ten years ago. He struggled with his own mortgage and credit card debt—just like many Americans, which made him a perfect credit counselor. Giving back was like going to anger management for him.

"Great to meet you. I did vote for you," said Abe.

"Thank you. I'm looking forward to putting this loan modification behind me," Harry said.

"You get to go to credit counseling, and the people who caused your financial hardship are on a golf course," Abe told Harry. "I'm here to give you information on how your home crisis was manufactured by banks and our government. This will help you make better future credit decisions.

"Your loan modification form shows you have a Schibt Mortgage from Steptin Schibt Bank. What do you hope to get out of this counseling?"

"This is just another requirement for me in this yearlong process," Harry said. "I just want to get back on my feet and end this nightmare. I just want my mortgage loan modification. It's time I start my life over again. My mortgage is twice the value of my home. Nobody will modify my loan."

"OK, well, it might be best if we focus on your Schibt Mortgage," Abe said. "You are current on your payments and have excellent credit. Your credit report is spotless. You have been taken advantage of for simply wanting to own a home. Your piece of the American dream ended up financially destroying you. My credit counseling objective is for you to understand that you were scammed. Do you have any doubts about this?"

"Not at all. I'm enjoying this so far," said Harry.

"Now, how does our banking system work? Let's begin with how the banking industry is now owned by our government," Abe said. "Broke banks are given zero-interest loans with no credit check. They get free money, and you have to sit through a credit-counseling course for your loan modification requirement. Politicians and Wall Street should take my credit counseling course, not guys like you.

"It's important that I disclose my own mortgage situation. My mortgage is 70 percent more than the market value of my townhouse. There is no program for me. I am just to be a good slave to my mortgage, association fees, taxes, and insurance. I'm an adult and will take responsibility for getting screwed by Wall Street. We are supposed to be quiet, obedient servants to the banks. We sign the mortgage contract. This contract binds us to a system with no options but short sales, foreclosure, and bankruptcy.

"If you're going to scam Americans, do it on our largest purchase—our homes. This is an attack on the American Dream. No matter what the politicians say, nothing gets done. Nothing has been done for homeowners. Who will pick up the bill for their American Dream? Empty political promises cannot save our homes.

"This is our lesson today. Our government owns our banking system. They cannot afford to pay for mortgages that are underwater with all the foreclosures and short sales being absorbed into a depressed real estate market. It would take another bubble to get your home value back in your lifetime. 'Protect and preserve' has become 'crash and burn.' With Americans making lower wages and lacking jobs, real estate can't increase in value.

"Business and the rich can afford to buy politicians, but we are left broke. Many have had to spend their savings to survive. The job crisis, debt crisis, healthcare crisis, and getting-up-in-the-morning crisis have taken a toll. We need to rebuild, and politicians still need to lie to get our vote. These leaders get rich when leaving office, and they scam us again. Their friends and family get jobs while we suffer."

Abe paused and took a deep breath. "OK," he continued. "On to business. Finding a way out with a loan modification is a way for you to rebuild your life after the destruction of our financial system. Unaffordable middle class lifestyles are becoming difficult and impossible to maintain for many of us. We have done nothing wrong but get scammed by the Wall Street investment bankers. I used to be middle class, but I can't afford it anymore. Some of us are suffering through unemployment. I know what that is like. It takes two incomes in a household to survive. Business and government take more and more.

"Credit abuse begins with the Wall Street investment banks that took over our government. Their objective was to get and keep us in debt. Credit cards, auto loans, student loans, and mortgages keep us buried in debt. Wall Street has convinced our government that your credit abuses caused the US to go from a financial superpower to a super debtor nation."

He paused again and took a quick sip of coffee. "The Han Jahb Home Loan Modification and Credit Addiction Program requires me to cover the twelve-step credit addiction program. This is an important step for you to get back on your feet. This twelve-step program is based on flash crash conspiracy planning. This is where Wall Street steals as much as legally possible and sticks us with the bill. As an example, the October 2008 Flash Crash allowed Wall Street to evacuate quickly, while the middle class got destroyed. Because Wall Street owns our government, we hear things like 'helping Wall Street helps Main Street.' Nothing is done to help the middle class like you except this twelve-step credit addiction program:

"Step 1: You will not be able to keep your home with corporate welfare programs. Step 2: You will not be getting anything from government home insurance programs. Step 3: You will not get a bonus or commission from selling worthless mortgage-backed securities. Step 4: You will not cash in with enormous profits or stock options like Wall Street for securitizing your mortgage. Step 5: You will not profit from rebuilding our financial system. Step 6: You will not profit from your business competitors' being eliminated. Step 7: You will not be collecting on insurance policies on worthless securities. Step 8: You will not be getting zero-interest loans. Step 9: You will not be getting any of the $700 billion TARP funding or bailouts. Step 10: You will not be getting a seven-figure salary on Wall Street. Step 11: You will not be getting drunk and celebrating not going to jail for selling or insuring worthless securities. Step 12: You will be paying for everything.

"Consider yourself a survivor of this recovery program. The twelve-step Credit Addiction Program is for Wall Street to recover and for you to go screw yourself." Abe smiled, then continued, "Our government is addicted to debt spending to buy votes. Their arrogance and stupidity qualify them for the job. We were stupid and voted for them. Their debt is our debt.

12-STEP CREDIT ADDICTION PROGRAM

- You will not be able to keep your home with corporate welfare programs
- You will not be getting anything from government home insurance programs
- You will not get a bonus or commission from selling worthless mortgage-backed securities
- You will not cash in with enormous profits or stock options like Wall Street for securitizing your mortgage
- You will not profit from rebuilding our financial system
- You will not profit from your business competitors' being eliminated
- You will not be collecting on insurance policies on worthless securities
- You will not be getting zero-interest loans
- You will not be getting any of the $700 billion TARP funding or bailouts
- You will not be getting a seven-figure salary on Wall Street
- You will not be getting drunk and celebrating not going to jail for selling or insuring worthless securities
- You will be paying for everything

"At some point, our country will need to come to terms with all our debt problems. We need to consider the impact of shadow debt. Unfunded entitlement, pensions, and government debt at the local, state, and federal level will need to be paid by taxpayers. This is on top of their mortgages, credit cards, student loans, and personal loans. At some point people might realize they've been cheated for wanting what has become an unaffordable American Dream."

"A false sense of entitlement trapped many of us. Upward mobility has been shattered by home equity destruction and unemployment. Conspicuous consumption has now become being able to afford a car to live in!

"Our government protects legalized stealing, which destroyed the middle class. They are not held accountable, but you are. To have a lifetime of savings stolen from you by incompetent politicians who are just interested in making big corporations money, getting votes, and high-paying jobs after self-service is what they care about."

"It is with much regret that I must inform you that you have been declined for a loan modification. Your bank, Steptin Schibt Bank, does not give loan mods. Thank you," said Abe.

"Wait, I'm shocked," Harry said. "I can't believe this after a year of work."

"The people who should not have been helped got all the help," wise Abe said. "The ones getting the help are making sure you are getting no help because they own our government. This is why they get all the assistance our government could possibly provide. Nothing is being done for American families. Please contact your bank for more information. Good luck."

Harry was surprised and shocked as he drove to visit his parents before leaving for Washington, DC. It was eleven a.m., and his flight was at three p.m.

"How's wrecking your life going?" asked Harry's dad, Warren Brokass.

"I got screwed again. My mortgage modification was denied," Harry said.

Harry was sitting on the back porch with his parents. The swamp and blue sky were a beautiful sight. His parents had raised his sister and him in their mobile home. They had now lived there for over thirty-five years. Paying off their mobile home was one of the smartest things they'd ever done.

"You know, I'm not asking for much. I just want a loan modification and male breast reduction surgery," said Harry, laughing.

Harry's mom, Carol, chimed in. "Yes, that's our son. At least, you tried."

"I am proud of you," said Warren.

"We are having the gator you all caught last week," Carol said as she put the gator meat into the fryer. "I'm using a new batter."

"It's always excellent!" said Warren.

"Yes," said Harry.

"Did you get the airboat battery fixed? I can't believe we got cell coverage," said Harry.

"Oh, ya, it runs better than ever," said Warren.

"Can you boys not use a machine gun? I'm worried about contaminating the meat," said Carol.

"That was me. OK," said Harry.

"I will use the machine gun," Warren said, laughing. "I have a new laser scope to try." Warren finished his beer and got another from the outdoor refrigerator. "I have to ask: How can you keep affording a home here and in Washington?"

"I'm spending everything I make. We helped Wall Street for three years, but I'm not allowed to say how things are going to change," Harry said. "My next project is to get Super Congress to approve zero-interest loans for individuals and small businesses. These are the folks we should've helped in the first place. We helped Wall Street to save our own asses, and now we'll help individuals. Empowering consumers will ignite our economy again."

"You'll cause a war between real taxpayers and Wall Street," Warren said, cracking open a beer. "There is no way you're going to get this through Congress. Zero-interest loans to individuals isn't a concept that Congress will even be able to understand."

Harry said, "My home isn't worth anything. This market isn't looking any better. We're being made to eat the loss. Nothing has been done to help us. Laws are ignored for corporations while we're chained to underwater mortgages. If I were a bank, I would get all the free money I need. I've had it. I'm broke. Nothing has been done for my underwater mortgage. It's twice the value of my home. For three years now, it's been underwater. No help for me."

Warren went to the refrigerator again and handed Harry and Carol another beer. "We're going to have to help fix what is going wrong," he said. "I'll need your help with a few things. We need to approach this from another direction. We have nothing to lose if you want to do something drastic. Good jobs are tough to find, and our retirement might not exist, but we must do something. We can expect nothing but must voice our freedom of speech. They will continue to make stealing our money legal."

"I haven't had enough beer for you to go on like this," Harry said. "Seems you have some ideas for making changes."

"Now, I haven't gone crazy," Warren said. "I want to rob a bank, but not just any bank, and I need your help to do it. You're a politician now, and you know legal stealing. This'll be tricky and complicated. Wall Street has destroyed this country, and we must make them pay. I can't believe we've witnessed the middle class being destroyed in my lifetime. Somebody is going to pay, and it is not going to be us anymore. We are going to rob Steptin Schibt Bank the same way they robbed us."

"I'm going to make a martini because this is not a discussion for beer," Harry said as he walked to the fully stocked outdoor bar. "Let's think about this. Legally robbing a bank is possible. Being a politician makes me an expert on *that*."

"You are broke and have nothing to lose," Warren said. "They have allowed big business to steal our way of life. Our government is just too willing to do whatever business, special interests, and the wealthy want. They take our money and give us lies in return for our votes. They fool us into believing things will change. They completely ignore that part about 'protecting and preserving.' You have to rob them the way they robbed us."

"Do you know what's so sick about all this?" Harry asked. "Lies are taking our jobs and destroying us. If everything is a lie, what world are we living in? Their lies are to make us think life is good. They give us a reason to get out of bed and go to work, day in and day out."

"I know you're uncomfortable with this," Warren said, "but it is legal stealing. You're a politician, so this should come naturally to you. I just need insider information."

Harry paused for a second. "OK, I will let you know one thing. The president is pushing a major reform plan for his next State of the Union Speech. It's called the ZERO Plan, for zero-interest loans, easy debt refinancing, required minimum income tax, and one-time retirement withdrawal. This will hurt Wall Street."

"I'll think about it. This is about robbing them as they robbed us. Insider information is about timing," said Warren.

"Yes, but I know nothing about this," said Harry. "You are too honest to do anything with this."

"You boys better not go to jail, or I will kick your ass," said Carol.

"We need to financially destroy them as they did us. 'Too big to fail' means nothing. They're going to have to fight with the whole trailer...rr, mobile home park. They've run us into the ground by playing by their own rules. They did it legally, as we'll do.

Nobody would expect us to crawl out of the swamp to getter done."

"It's ready," said Carol, and everybody enjoyed the gator with fried okra and grits.

"Excellent as usual!" said Warren as he finished loading the cooler with beer. "Let's go play shuffleboard before your flight."

Day 2: How To Create a Successful FUC Plan by Dick Melong

It was Friday, January 6, 2012, when I met Dick Melong at the Scott Free Capitol Bar. He was about to provide training to newly elected members of Congress. Dick and I play golf at least two times a week. I had been concerned over his erratic behavior of not keeping on speaking points. Everybody considered him a senior do-nothing leader. To get anything done, Dick was needed. His big dream was to become a pro golfer, and having a flexible, part-time job with excellent benefits allowed him to pursue his dream.

Two days ago in the early evening, Dick was alone, finishing eighteen holes on the course that abutted his home. He could see lightning in the distance. Dick's hands were sweaty, and he had trouble getting a grip when he swung hard. There was a bright flash, and lightning destroyed his favorite driver. He cried for twenty minutes, trying to find his way home in excruciating pain. All of us thought he was never the same after that.

I shook hands with Dick and said, "What is it with the shaved head?"

"Like it? I lost a bet with my son. I think I am going to keep it," said Dick as I got a mimosa.

"You look like a skinhead," I said.

"My wife likes touching it. I better get started," Dick said as he spiked his coffee and went to the podium. "Thank you for an opportunity to speak here this morning. Please help yourself to the food and drinks at the full bar.

"I am sure you all noticed that my friend of over twenty years is here, Goldballs'n Sak. He will be by the bar if you would like to meet the next president of the United States.

"I don't know why I stand here today after being struck by lightning. My life's goal must now be to pass on the power of F Politics. The things I have done are for the good of our nation, but I am only one man. It is time to pass on the knowledge of F Planning. This will be my first speech in which I do not blame the other party for my own weaknesses. It is time I own up. The financial hardship in our country has been the fault of our government playing F Politics.

"Our topic today will be How to Create a Successful F-U-C Plan. This is what our country is built on. I am the best there is at creating these plans. As a politician who has not accomplished anything for American families, I know what I am talking about.

"I don't know why I am not in jail. I got into politics to hide from the law. The healthcare company I founded paid the largest fine ever for fraud. I paid billions in fines for committing Medicare bill processing fraud. I broke all the records and did not go to jail. This whole country is falling apart while I play golf.

"I have to share the highest level of strategic planning available. This is something that touches all of our lives. It has the potential for real, powerful change. To have a bright future, it is important for our party to support proven and reliable strategic F Plans.

F Politics describes high-level initiatives to get things done. The core is a F-U-C Plan. That's pronounced *fuc*." The audience chuckled. "F-U-C stands for Face Unfortunate Consequences. It is easy to write a FUC Plan. You create a phrase that starts with the letters F, U, and C. It's that simple.

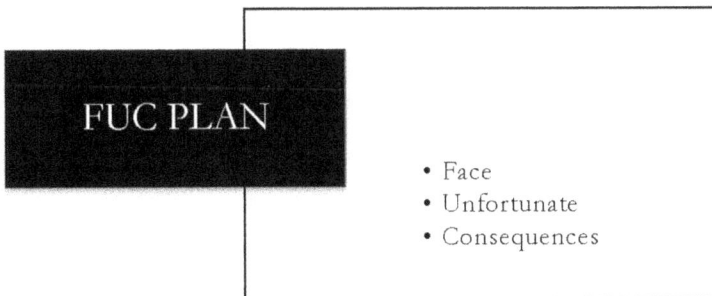

FUC PLAN

- Face
- Unfortunate
- Consequences

Here's one of my all-time favorites, and it destroyed the world financial system: Free cash, Unbelievable risk taking, and Complicated processes. Each phrase relates to a common purpose or objective. It is simple and powerful. Let me be clear: FUC Plans are to manipulate voter sheep, disseminate lies, steal wealth, and cause destruction in place of protect and preserve. Politicians pick the winners and losers, and the middle class is losing.

"Let's break down the Flash Crash FUC Plan. Free cash to business has caused us to go broke. The subsidies, tax breaks, favorable regulations, bailouts, stimulus, and free loans are causing enormous debt. The US Treasury gives zero-interest loans to large corporations and not to struggling homeowners. Let's not forget that the people who sold worthless securities made huge profits and saw increased stock value, salaries, and bonuses before the October 2008 crash. During the rebuilding of our financial system, they still make huge profits and see increased stock value, salaries, and bonuses. Let us be clear whom we helped. It was not American families. Many people who were formerly middle class think we are really in the second Great Depression.

FLASH CRASH FUC PLAN

- Free cash
- Unbelievablle risk taking
- Complicated processes

"Unbelievable risk taking by businesses is made possible by our government. Wall Street has the ability to gamble with no risk. Deceptive banks, insurance, and brokerage firms can make money with taxpayers guaranteeing the bet. It is unbelievable and inexcusable that the American people allowed this to occur. As politicians, we cannot say much because we have, in essence, legalized stealing.

"Capitalism should not come with a guarantee. Imagine going to Las Vegas and having your losses guaranteed by the federal government. That is win-win. Our government takes on business risks and nationalizes losses. When there's no risk, banks lend to anybody. That fuels lending to unqualified buyers. The existing regulations that could have prevented this were not enforced because red tape hinders business growth.

"And last, complicated processes cover up and hide the legalizing stealing. Securitizing fraud mortgages and selling them as high-grade investments imploded our global financial system. Complex regulations mixed with enigmatic corporations and incentives to fail make oversight and governance a monumental and impossible task.

"Struggling homeowners were not bailed out like Wall Street. Our government guaranteed worthless, fraudulent mortgages. Homeowners were guaranteed nothing. Wall Street gets all the cash they need. In exchange, politicians get campaign money and jobs when they leave office. The process has to be so complicated that no reasonable person can figure it out. Keeping government simple enough for all of us to understand protects our freedom.

"With the US government watching out for banks by nationalizing losses and recapitalizing their business, reckless investing can continue with no obstacles. American families will continue to be ignored. Not providing these kinds of loans or loan modifications to American families could eventually cause unrest. They might even wake up and figure out they have been losing a class war for thirty years. How we convinced them to vote for us when we do nothing for them, I will never understand.

"Now, FUC Plans are multi-dimensional. One FUC Plan can be supported by multiple FUC Plans. Many politicians, for instance, use the Fantabulous Access FUC Plan to support F Politics.

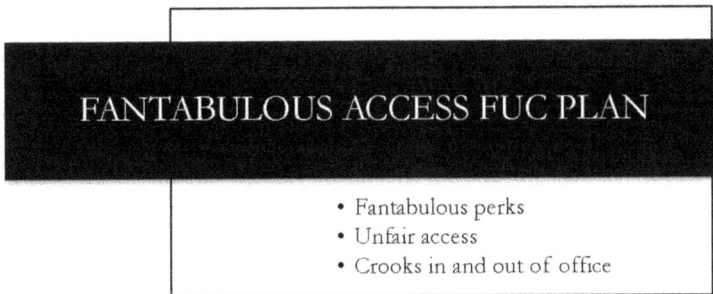

FANTABULOUS ACCESS FUC PLAN

- Fantabulous perks
- Unfair access
- Crooks in and out of office

"The *F* is for the fantabulous perks provided to Super Congress World. Politicians have a lot of free time with their part-time positions and need to plan the most incredible golf trips with the resources provided by lobbyists and special interests. These groups are eager to take us on private planes anywhere in the world to get tax favors, subsidies, stimuli, bailouts, and favorable regulations.

"The *U* is for unfair access, which is demanded of politicians if they want campaign cash. Business is buying favorable legislation. Super Congress is paid for by the well connected and rich. Super Congress is where real business gets done, and you do not need to deal with the broke public. Our employers—these giant corporations, not the public—expect us to get it done without anybody understanding or even conceiving that they own our government. Just the fact they own us means they are above the law.

"And finally, *C*: crooks in and out of office. They keep the system working. This is a must because eventually we will be thrown out and need to flee to a seven-figure job.

"Does everything we do involve F Politics? Yes, because you need to know if you're getting screwed or you are screwing yourself. This is knowledge vital to our survival. At some point, you realize that an F Plan is working you over. This workshop is to at least help you figure out if the bus is backing up over you, because I doubt your drunken ass can drive the bus. Even if you can drive, you will drive all of us over a cliff.

"Does anybody have any questions?"

I was shocked at what I was hearing and ordered a Long Island iced tea. Dick was definitely not himself. Everybody in the room was just looking at one another, as they did not want to ask the crazy man a question.

Then some young kid, a Senator, whose mom had probably driven him here, raised his hand and asked, "I signed a pledge saying that I would never, ever raise taxes. Is this a FUC Plan?"

Everybody could feel the tension in the room as Dick took a deep breath as he thought before he said, "When you are planning a wild sex orgy, is it important to have an odd or even number of friends? You need to know this to be successful in this town. Signing that pledge is as effective as slamming your balls in a car door. All of you are millionaires. Nobody is going to raise our taxes. The former middle class and the poor need to pay our taxes so we can get tax cuts. If they don't have the money to pay their taxes, then the money must be borrowed. This is causing tax disparity as we get wealthy. Economists have labeled this a tax orgy. Overall tax revenues decrease as our wealth increases because we pay little or no taxes. We are the rich, who must protect the rich. Our tax orgy must be protected by a political party blockade to make sure this does not change. If the former American middle class need to whore themselves out to pay for our tax orgy, who cares?

"It is an honor to have Goldballs'n Sak here today. I recently read an article on his enormous accumulation of wealth since 2008. His net worth has gone from $7 billion to $45 billion today. The wealth of working American families has decreased because it is in his pocket. Our government even borrowed money to make sure his wealth increased. It is vital to our democracy to support Goldballs'n Sak as president. The game must go on screwing the non-millionaire voter sheep for us to stay in office.

"American families are broke and deeply in debt. They are struggling to pay their bills, and they are lucky to have a job. The misrepresentations of investment securities and market manipulation destroy the middle class. Real regulations would be tragedy for Wall Street with our rigged capitalism. Because Americans cannot pay millions to attorneys and lobbyists, their silent obedience is expected.

"Our local, state, and federal governments are all borrowing to keep up spending levels. Nothing can fill the void of a broke consumer. Revenue is down with the destruction of the middle class. Less money is being collected from property taxes because of plummeting home values. High unemployment and lower-paying jobs are impacting tax collections. With less tax revenue, our government borrows and does not tax the rich, while the middle class is gone. We are in complete denial that we are broke. Their spending and more spending is destroying our country. Deficits continue to go up while we remain in denial.

"All of us know that you cannot pay for your life by putting it on a credit card except if somebody else is paying your credit card bill. Here, the people paying your bills just need you to vote them into office. Politicians have hit the credit limit. No planning or action is being done to become debt free. Destroying the middle class was not enough. Future generations will become debt slaves because of the lack of effective, meaningful leadership.

"F Politics, or FUC Planning, is fundamentally changing our economy. Our capitalistic society cannot operate without risk taking, which is a component of our entrepreneurial spirit. Making our government take on business risk is undermining this entrepreneurial spirit. Covering the losses involved in this risk taking is not for us to do as taxpayers. Nationalizing business losses is destroying our economy. Our government is not paying for the loss in your home equity. This legal stealing must end if we are to rebuild.

"Politicians are just as responsible as the Wall Street crooks. Borrowing and gambling with our money must end. Our government's lack of enforcement makes politicians accomplices to the crimes. This is why there will be no jail sentences—because it is too complicated to figure out what a worthless security is and what party is at fault. As politicians, we are just as evil as the crooks for protecting them, just to rebuild the financial systems they destroyed.

"All political parties work FUC Plans. For years, our central focus has been creating a better future with F Politics. From the time you get up in the morning until you go to bed, FUC Plans impact every aspect of your life. Our dedication and commitment to maintaining unquestioned power over the American people relies directly to our ability to command F Politics.

"F Politics is the only solution we offer to lost and broken American families that we use to get votes. Your ability to stay in office is directly related to how well you master FUC Planning. Our economy will collapse if we do not commit to solid FUC Plans. It is time for you to provide leadership on sound and proven F Politics. Thank you!"

I shook a lot of hands and took pictures with everybody before going to play golf with Dick. Our golf clubs and drinks were ready when we arrived at my company's course, called the Steptin Schibt Capitol Golf Course.

"Your speech got under my skin. Do you think it is appropriate to teach how to screw over voters?" I said as we went to the first tee.

"That was a crowd of amateurs," said Dick.

"You make me want to switch political parties," I said.

"You play both sides, so that would be easy," said Dick as he drove a beautiful swing. "We can't have our party destroyed again like Butch and Chainsaw. You will be lucky to get any votes."

I said, "I disagree. We are shutting down voting for many in the other party. Our democracy is shutting down our most privileged honor. Whoever gets to vote will be filtered to vote for me. I will win no matter what. Let's also not forget who owns Super Congress World."

Day 3: Super Congress World: User's Manual

Super Congress World was my greatest accomplishment. It has enormous influence over guiding and shaping our daily lives. Powerful legislation created a world of privilege and access for a chosen few. The human race has never been the same since the US Congress created the Super Congress World Law.

Becoming president of the United States would not be possible for me without the secret creation of this incredibly lavish facility. Super Congress World was built under the US Capitol Visitor Center, which is attached to the US Congress. It was completed in December 2008. Americans could now visit Congress and experience congressional gridlock, incompetence, finger pointing, and blame like in their living room. The Visitor Center was perfect for concealing the world built below.

Because I helped design the facilities, I enjoyed providing tours to newly elected freshmen. I intimately understood the special requirements of elected officials and enjoyed referring to them as my bitches.

On a cold and snowing Friday, January 13, 2012, I started a tour for twelve official bitches. "Please come this way through security to the underground levels. As you saw, the Visitor Center is above us on the first three underground floors. We are walking private, underground floors. This is the Grand Lodge Atrium, which is four stories underground within the complex. If you look down, you can see the golf course and fountains on the bottom. The finest craftsmen and materials were used to create each level of this underground labyrinth.

"Our tour today will be on levels four through seven. We are on level four, the Scott Free Capitol Bar. Below that is level five, the Han Jahb Capitol Spa. Next is level six, the Dick Melong Capitol Bathhouse. The lowest level, level seven, is the Steptin Schibt Capitol Golf Course. I am happy to welcome you to Super Congress World!

SUPER CONGRESS WORLD

- Level 4: Scott Free Capitol Bar
- Level 5: Han Jahb Capitol Spa
- Level 6: Dick Melong Capitol Bathhouse
- Level 7: Steptin Schibt Capitol Golf Course

"We built this complex to have special access to power. It is a way to escape the responsibility and criticism of the world above. This abyss was created as an incredibly privileged way to spend the day. Have a drink; enjoy the spa and bathhouse, and good luck making it to the golf course.

"This facility is easy to get into and out of because we insisted that it be drunk friendly. We are now in the lobby of Scott Free Capitol Bar. There are many different bars and restaurant sections on this floor, all with private meeting rooms. The most popular are the ones with stripper poles. You can see the twenty-foot 3D screens here. Other bars are for sports, news, or porn. You will need a special smartphone app to listen to the screen of your choice.

"This floor is for all political parties, lobbyists, and special interests. Present and former politicians are welcome here. This is the only floor in Super Congress that allows all political parties. This is where you become better politicians.

"Let's walk over here to the sports bar, where I can show you the touch screens for ordering drinks and food. First, press here and look at the screen, so the facial recognition scanner can identify you. Second, the screen shows you the five drinks you have ordered most frequently, and you can hit a quick button here to order your usual. Here are the menus. Please flip through them and choose a drink. Then, you have to select the special interest group or lobbyist that will be billed. Make your selection and press 'done' here to complete your order. Now you've actually accomplished something today.

"Also, these ordering screens are found on all floors. The golf course has two bars for each tee, and you will need to wait to be served before moving the next tee. There are two house drinks that are completely free. Steptin Schibt Bank pays for these drinks, so you will not need to select a special interest or lobbyist to pay. These drinks are the Seven-inch and the Ramrod. A double is called the Seven-inch Ramrod. Please feel free to have all the Seven-inch Ramrods you want. It is the best thing you've ever had. You can easily order three doubles in a row by selecting 777 Gang Bang on the touch screen here. Within one minute, you will be served. Tips are no longer allowed because one political party kept saying they did not have cash. A 20 percent minimum tip is added when we bill your special interest group. If you need help, touch this help square. You will be directed to a helpful assistant in India. Let's order!

"I need a Seven-inch Ramrod. Notice how the facial recognition recognizes me. I touch here. It is that easy," I said while my drink was brought out.

"I have to try this," said some bitch.

"See, it recognizes you. Now select a drink here."

"I want a Manhattan!" said the bitch. "How did it already have a Manhattan as my favorite?"

"The chief of staff in your office has set everything up for you," I said. "Press here and your hot wings will be served shortly."

Her drink came out along with wings as everybody else enjoyed ordering.

"This Ramrod is excellent! What's in it?" asked a bitch.

"I have perfected the world's finest vodka. It has pomegranate and my vodka," I said.

"I could get addicted to this. I'm ready for another Seven-inch Ramrod," said some bitch.

"Me too," said a few bitches.

"How do we order a round of shots?" asked another bitch.

"When you press the drink menu, touch this box that lists the top shots we offer or press custom here to type in your request. I will order a round. Here you put in how many shots," I said.

The shots came out quickly.

"Cheers," said everybody as we raised our glasses.

"Please help yourself to the Spread Eagle Buffet, courtesy of my bank. Anytime you see an ice sculpture with food, it is free, courtesy of Steptin Schibt Bank. You have to try the freshly baked bagel with deep-fried chitlins and lobster tail. We will be covering a few major topics today, so you will need a drink. Let's get started after everybody orders."

"How do I order food?" asked a bitch.

"Just press the food menu here. Scroll through it like this. Ox balls wrapped in bacon looks good. Just touch it, and now we select the special interest. It will be out shortly," I said.

"This is fun," said another bitch.

"Please try these ox balls," I said.

"These are the best balls I have ever had," said a bitch.

"If everybody is ready, let's go to the meeting room to the left here," I said. "This is my favorite meeting room. Try not to fall asleep in the big leather chairs as I often do." Everybody relaxed and was ready.

"The strength of democracy comes from its ability to change and adapt over time. Super Congress World is one of the most secret initiatives ever enacted by an ostensibly democratic government. It was created to fill the void of what was not getting done by the executive, legislative, and judicial branches.

"Debt is so out of control that secret oversight is warranted. Super Congress World is a shadow government that can ignore laws and regulations that hinder growth and real profits. Most Americans are chained with debt and must have their cash fix. Those who control the cash control the people. Super Congress derives its power from using the financial system to control our nation's wealth.

"Super Congress World was created for two reasons. Number one is to take people's paychecks. Number two is to create the illusion of not taking their paychecks. Why do you think we bought this place? Super Congress World protects and preserves this illusion. Incompetence and lying are the only things shared equally by all political parties. We must make sure the truth does not get out and support the illusion of dedication and commitment to improving the lives of American families.

"Business and Super Congress World claim a portion of everyone's paycheck. Super Congress World collects taxes when people pay their business bills and when businesses take money from them. Through unfair and invisible tax schemes, we collect taxes on paychecks and on the spending of them. To accomplish this, we use the Getting-Your-Ass-Waxed FUC Plan—fixed cash flow, unreasonable costs and fees, and chaining Americans to contract obligations.

GETTING-YOUR-ASS-WAXED FUC PLAN

- Fixed cash flow
- Unreasonable costs and fees
- Chaining Americans to contract obligations

"How do we control spending? Fixed cash flow controls business and government activity. Business must always be backed above regular people for us to extort the most money. Everything is based on getting Americans contractually bound. It is vital to make sure the law is on the side of business so we can squeeze people for every dime. Super Congress World legally makes sure of it. You sign a contract and are stuck in debt for years. A mortgage is the perfect example. You are obligated to pay a certain sum over a certain period of time. This assures us fixed portions of your paycheck every month.

"Unreasonable costs and fees are involved in locking you into contract obligations. With a mortgage you are locked into a credit report fee, origination fee, appraisal fee, recording fee, escrow fee, title insurance, document preparation fee, attorneys' fees, property inspection fee, underwriting fee, property insurance, and taxes. You signed the contract, which allows us to make you pay and pay more. Also, you'd better pay taxes and insurance extortion for the life of the contract.

"I have mentioned mortgages here to explain that our economy is still broken because our largest industry, real estate, is still being neglected by our government. This is hurting our growth. My company gets record profits from the support of corporate welfare. Wall Street has gotten government help, but Main Street has been neglected with no mortgage relief from home equity being stolen. Nothing in our economy will be stabilized until struggling homeowners are helped. Homeowners have become debt slaves.

"Chaining Americans to contract obligations is an integral part of our financial stability. A piece of everyone's freedom is lost when a contract is signed. Somebody else now owns a portion of his or her paychecks. Monthly bills are the same way. Your phone bills, utility bills, childcare costs, car insurance, and health insurance are all costs that claim a portion of your paycheck. Controlling American families is necessary for the rich to get richer. Making Americans debt slaves is how we steal their wealth.

"Super Congress World transfers taxpayers' wealth to businesses and the rich legally. Certain things must be done to protect the illusion of not stealing people's paychecks. We accomplish this with the Parrot FUC Plan—follow along with speaking points, ugly truths must be avoided, and constantly avoiding real action.

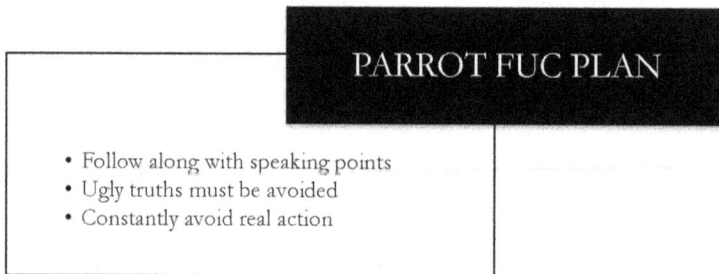

PARROT FUC PLAN

- Follow along with speaking points
- Ugly truths must be avoided
- Constantly avoid real action

"This is important: Follow along with talking points to hide the truth. The truth is what we say it is. Super Congress World is reality. Talking points create an illusion. This illusion supports and shapes the businesses that we protect and preserve to steal paychecks.

"As elected officials, you are fortunate to have part-time jobs where incompetence and lying are acceptable. Staying in office requires only repeating the right buzzwords and talking points to create the appearance of looking smart and actually caring about something other than yourself. If that fails, try vote buying. Super Congress World was made to accomplish this.

"Ugly truths must be avoided for you to stick to your talking points. These talking points may be lies, but you need to accept them as the only truth. It is disloyalty to not keep on the party message. This is a necessary evil to your party's survival. Deviating from the script will jeopardize your reelection and campaign cash.

"When your party sends an e-mail on what to say, follow it blindly. Do not try to think for yourself because this will be disloyal to your party. When your party says the same thing over and over again, it appears to the public that we are strong and unified. What you think does not matter. Your talking points will be in line with what the businesses, special interests, and lobbyists that fund your campaigns want. They create these talking points. Your talking points are the only leadership you will get or need.

"Constantly avoiding real action ensures that nothing will be accomplished. Some of you will be obstructionist and just say no, no, no to everything. This is called getting paid to do nothing. Just make sure you keep on message. You can do whatever you want as long as you can blame the other party. Constant blaming and doing nothing has become the norm. Important issues get ignored, and the legal stealing continues. If you expect to get anything accomplished other than reelection, you do not belong in Super Congress World.

"I cannot stress enough the importance of keeping on message. Sounding like parrots by saying the same thing makes you appear powerful because your party will have one voice. It creates an illusion of safety and security for non-millionaires. You are paid to say talking points, not the truth.

"You need to prove yourself to us. Down here in Super Congress World, the US Congress above us is referred to as the temp agency. You are all temps working for us. If you prove yourself with the right skills, and you are a complete sociopath, there are many lucrative opportunities. Can you believe the full-time pay and benefits with full pension with your part-time temp jobs?

"Super Congress is important and necessary for our economy to grow. Businesses became so greedy that they destroyed themselves, and Super Congress World now owns it. Many Americans are now broke from Wall Street's worthless securities. Super Congress World stole cash, homes, and dreams to make sure the illusion of hope remains. Super Congress World did not, however, make sure that American families had enough money to pay their bills. Corporations and the rich were helped, not American families.

"The ambiguous Super Congress World creates many questions: Could you destroy the wealthiest country that ever existed and be too arrogant and inept to know it? Super Congress World solves this dilemma by creating a place to hide and prevent real action for American families. With unlimited resources, Super Congress World is free to create an illusion of protecting and preserving. Power allows the truth to be covered up. Super Congress World decides what the truth is. Hiding Americans from the truth is protecting them.

"Super Congress World is our special happy place, but we do have work to do. The interest group that paid for your drinks, spa treatments, food, and golf will show up here, depending on what arrangements you've made. They can just send you an e-mail, text, or call. If you want to get reelected, this is where you'll need to be. There are unlimited resources here.

"Let's now try to find our way to level five, the Han Jahb Capitol Spa. It is mandated in the law that created Super Congress World that levels five, six, and seven be separated into two identical facilities for both major parties. Each has its own separate, identical facilities. If you don't belong to either of the two major parties, you must decide whom to caucus with.

"Our focus here is to give current and former elected officials a safe place to relax away from the stress of serving at their part-time positions. Levels five, six, and seven were created as politics-free areas for you to work out and take a break. Cell phones and computers are not allowed in the bathhouse. We have gone out of our way to keep both major political parties separate. Businesses, interest groups, and the rich pay to keep political parties separate to hide their identities. It is inconceivable to expect you to be able to relax while being attacked and blamed by members of other political parties. No staffers who work in your office are allowed in the spa and bathhouse, and especially not during nude golfing days.

"I don't know about you, but I could use another Seven-inch Ramrod," I said.

"I am ready for it," some bitch said while trying the touch screen.

"Do politicians really spend a lot of time here?" some bitch asked while we walked to the main hall.

"Yes, the house drink is highly addictive, and politicians are always looking for freebies. This privileged complex is subtly enticing," I said as we went onto the down escalator to level 5.

"Where is the bathroom?" asked some bitch.

"You will find it around the corner here. All our bathrooms are extravagant and coed. The attendants do not expect a tip and are well paid." I said. Everybody checked out the restroom as I waited at the spa main entrance.

While we walked into the spa, I said "The Sand Box FUC Plan includes fun and relaxation, unmatched massage therapies, and complete fitness facilities.

SAND BOX FUC PLAN

- Fun and relaxation
- Unmatched massage therapies
- Complete fitness facilities

"Fun and relaxation were the objectives of creating this spa. It is important for us to meet everybody's needs. Our entire facility is handicap and drunk friendly.

"Unmatched massage therapies and a tanning salon are down the hall here. This is where I go for my spray tan. There are eighty professional massage therapists available to provide you with a wide selection of massages and many other great indulgences. My favorite is the Drill-Baby-Drill Colonic.

"Everything here is free. The spa is busiest in the morning before golf. My favorite massages are the Tie-Me-Up and Hide-The-Zucchini. Your massage technicians can be male, female, bisexual, or even Swedish cheerleaders. Our computer system already knows your age and alleged sexual orientation, and can be adjusted to meet your special needs.

"Complete fitness facilities are right this way, but who cares? I am always too drunk for that. Well, if working out does interest you, we are proud to have the latest equipment. Free personal trainers are available from five a.m. to nine p.m. Towels, water, and vodka are provided at the doors. Racquetball and tennis courts are by the bowling alley, and the running track is to the left here.

"Yoga classes are done in these rooms. We have the best Irish yoga—better known as drunk yoga—every day at ten a.m.

"Both parties share this section of the spa. Please come this way to the *Let the Eagle Soar* statue, which shows a map of this entire incredible floor. Many of you will enjoy the health benefits of bondage in the Eagle Claw Bipartisan Bondage Pavilion to our right. You are welcome to customize your sessions, or you can make a selection on the touch screens. You have to try the Eagle Claw, but my secret pleasure is Pole Dancing Without Spilling Your Drink. You can also bring in your own gear.

"The Birds of Prey Bipartisan Gift Shop has an extensive collection of personal care products. All lingerie and leather clothing are tailored. We have an hour turnaround time.

"Next to the gift shop, you will see the Midlife Crisis Tattoo Shop. We are fortunate to have the some of the world's finest tattoo artists. You will have to make an appointment because of the backlog. On Tattoo Tuesdays, we have free drinks and piercings, along with strippers with tattoos and a bondage show.

"Let's get a refill at the bar here. You will not believe the great service. I have to let you know that all the employees at Super Congress World are illegal aliens. If they complain, we deport them, so please enjoy their services. There have been complaints about having illegals down here, but we do whatever we want to exploit this underground tax-free economy, as long as they do whatever we tell them to. Most of the stuff we do is illegal anyway, so officials have fallen in line. You temps know who is boss.

"The Dick Melong Capitol Bathhouse is down this way, to Level 6. "As you can see, these columns are a rare imported purple marble, and the top is solid gold. The chandeliers were custom made in France and can support adult weight. This right here is the largest indoor Roman water facility ever created. The Roman buffet is courtesy of the Foundation for Drowning Americans in Underwater Mortgages. The two Olympic-size pools are way over here by the waterfalls.

"My favorite bar in this entire complex is in the center of the bathhouse this way," I said as we walked to an area where you could see in. "You need to have a towel or bathing suit on while on this floor. As you can see, this bar is called 'Going To Rehab'. Now you know what we mean when we say we are 'Going To Rehab'. It has a friendly Caribbean theme with actual beach sand from the Virgin Islands. We bring in a lot of great DJ's. This is one of the largest bars in the world. You can come here anytime 24/7 because Super

Congress World never closes, even on holidays. I will be here after golfing. As you can see, our friends are here."

"There is Dick Melong, Butch, and Chainsaw over there," said some bitch.

"Yes. It is crowded. Look at the strippers. Beautiful!" I said.

"Can I bring my wife?" asked some bitch.

"Only on Stripper Swinger Saturdays. I will be here with my wife around one a.m.," I said.

"I have to show you where the maze is. We used to have orgies on Thursday and Saturday only. Because the drunks complained about wanting more sex, this maze was built. You will find plenty of action in there 24/7. You will make a lot of political connections here," I said.

"There are also Roman saunas and steam rooms to explore this way. The saunas have stripper poles, but we had to take them out of the steam rooms because of injuries. I really miss having them in the steam room, but some idiot broke his ribs flying off of it. By the way, I know who got hurt, and I'm pretty sure his injury was the product of some rather rough sex. We know how politicians enjoy poles, after all.

"The Nile River Tube Ride runs along the perimeter. It runs really rough from five a.m. to eleven a.m. for kayaking, and smooth the rest of the day for drunk tubing. The large tubes can handle up to seven but many more if they are on top of you. Nudity is technically not allowed on the water slides for safety, so please wear at least a jock strap, though anybody riding on top of you can be nude.

"As you can see, nudity is allowed and, in fact, required for lobbyists and special interests. We do provide private rooms for you to seal the deal. This way is the lavish private meeting rooms that we have just expanded. We initially had one hundred rooms, but the drunks insisted we add additional rooms to keep our country's business private. As of this week, we have three hundred rooms. Your special interest or lobbyist is charged five hundred dollars an hour, so you better be providing plenty of favors and special treatment to enjoy this area. The rooms have different themes.

"Our company has our own room that I can show you right here. This is similar to a lavish hotel room that is about four thousand square feet. You don't have to worry about hidden cameras or microphones because security inspects each room after each meeting. The bed can support twenty along with the hot tub. We went for classy, modern, sleek furniture and classic tiles in the bathroom where the bar is. There are forty showerheads. All rooms have a fireplace. That was my wife's idea. She did the decorating."

"It's beautiful!" said a bitch as others showed approval.

"Thank you," I said. "Now level seven is to the escalators this way. Welcome to the Steptin Schibt Capitol Golf Course. This is the largest indoor golf course complex ever created. This secret hologram technology does not exist in the real world. This is the greatest benefit ever provided to temps in the history of the world. Wherever you look here, you will find a free bar. Admission is by invitation only. You must invite special interests, lobbyists, and the rich. Whoever you invite to the party must pay. Let's not forget why we are here. Good luck to Americans struggling to get a job in this F Plan economy.

"Weather problems will not ruin the day here. Seal the deal here or in the bathhouse. The hologram creates this environment to protect us from global warming. These are live trees and grass, but the sky and horizon are created by the hologram. We change the course every month. We used to do this every week, but the drunks complained.

"Each party has its own sections; there are four eighteen-hole golf courses for both major parties. The underground of Washington, DC has become a golf course. We know how to live and live better. It is snowing and cold outside, but look at this incredible world down here.

"Notice that the golf carts hover above the ground, and nobody is driving. This is to prevent drunk driving. Our super computers automatically control them on magnetic pathways. You just have to press start, and they will stop at the next tee. They are equipped with a full surround sound stereo, four TVs, and ordering screens. The leather seats are even heated and have massage settings.

"My favorite golf day, by the way, is Naked Friday Golfing with Strippers on Trampolines."

"I was wondering about the nudity," said a bitch.

"Try to do that in your home district," I said, smiling. "This facility is a secret because of the great hardship being endured by the American public. Some think that Super Congress World is the seed to our destruction. They think we are destroying ourselves. That is un-American and must be silenced. Please enjoy Super Congress World. I need to get golfing now. Cheers and thank you."

Day 4: Wall Street Annual Corporate Welfare Extortion Awards Luncheon to Celebrate Profiting on the Great Depression II by Harry Brokass

On Tuesday, January 17, 2012, Han Jahb, CEO of Steptin Schibt Bank, played golf with Harry Brokass before the Wall Street Annual Corporate Welfare Extortion Awards Luncheon at twelve p.m. The lunch was at this time because nothing got done in Washington DC with my vodka after two p.m.

There were actually politicians whom Han could not buy with sports tickets, golfing junkets, or employment. Harry Brokass was actually ethical, which continued to frustrate Han. As the Financial Services Committee chairman, Harry could influence significant legislation or ignore it.

"Great to see you," Han said as they shook hands. It was eight a.m. as he sat having a mimosa at the first tee at the Steptin Schibt Capitol Golf Course at Super Congress World.

"I think I will have the same," said Harry.

"How are you doing?" Han said.

"Things could be better. I am glad we could play today before the awards lunch," Harry said. "I almost hit a car today with the ice on the road. Look, I'm shaking." Harry held up his shaking hand.

"It is always sunny down here," Han said, smiling.

"I have to let you know that your bank denied my mortgage loan modification," Harry said.

"Really? I didn't know you needed one."

"There is no reason why I should need your help. The entire process woke me up," Harry said. He started moving toward the cart, and Han followed. Harry teed off first.

"You should have let me know. I would have given you a legitimate mortgage and not our usual junk financing," Han said.

"That's not how I operate. Your bank must work for more than just the well connected. This is just another banking scam. Screwing over the American public with scam loans and your outrageous fees is going to bite you in the ass because I am going to make sure of it," Harry said as they got into the cart.

"I run a business. It is vitally important for me to have record short-term profits to get my bonus," said Han.

"Some of us cannot afford certain things in life. I do not get corporate welfare like you. Some of us have to make an honest living," Harry said.

"You need to remember who you really work for," Han said. "Wall Street owns Super Congress World."

"Do you think voters will figure out that our banking system no longer exists?" Harry asked. "Our government is the only real bank. Crooks like you haven't gone to jail because I am playing golf with you!"

"We have been lucky to have such great friends," said Han, with a slight, knowing smile.

Harry wasn't amused. "You know, I don't know what your company does. Are you a bank, a hedge fund, a law firm, or a placement agency for politicians? You are bigger than ever. Wall Street is too complicated to fairly tax and regulate. We cannot keep ignoring the theft of people's homes and retirements. Wall Street gets free loans, bailouts, and stimulus while voters receive nothing in return."

"I will admit that our financial system melted down in October 2008," Han said. "Our fraudulent lending, worthless securities, and theft of retirement funds annihilated the middle class."

They putted into the hole and moved forward to the second tee.

"Ordinary people think we are stupid," Harry said. "We make them think they are in control. This comfort gives them even less control. They think they are smarter than us. We control our economy, but they think they know what is going on. To challenge it, they would have to challenge their own thought processes, so they won't do it."

"I don't know what you're talking about," Han told him. "Congress created the legislation that defines how we do business. I need your support because you are on the Financial Services Committee. This is why you are hosting the awards lunch today."

Harry said, "We gave you everything because we believed that helping Wall Street would also help Main Street. I think we can agree that Main Street was screwed."

"I can assure you that Main Street's retirement money and bank accounts are safe and sound because we own Super Congress World. We protect the American Dream of home ownership—unless we can make more money without it." Han smiled.

"You admit it because you know you will do whatever you want and just pay the settlement," Harry said. He got out his driver.

Han said to Harry, "Your man tits are ruining your swing."

"There is no way you can be making fun of my rack," Harry snapped. "I am tired of telling you it's muscle!" Harry put away his driver and went to Han's clubs and said, "This is a really sweet custom driver. This must have cost what? 7,000 or $10,000. See! These are chest muscles." Harry bent the driver and threw it in the lake. "It's a complete custom set." Harry was smiling as he threw the rest of the clubs into the lake.

"What are you doing? Have you lost it?" Han said.

"I owe you a settlement for damaging your $100,000 clubs. Accept this dollar as settlement," Harry took a dollar out of his wallet and threw it at Han. "This is what you do. I will see you at lunch!" Harry said loudly, walking away smiling.

Han stood in shock. He then climbed into the golf cart and pressed cancel on the touch screen. Han went to the 'Going to Rehab' bar at Dick Melong Capitol Bathhouse and laughed with his friends about the incident.

Goldballs'n Sak received warning messages on his smartphone when the computer programs that monitored Super Congress World recognized unusual behavior, meetings, or conversations that could have significant political consequences. He could replay this political intelligence at his convenience on his smartphone, tablet, or computer. He could watch and listen in on all areas of the complex, and nobody was aware he had this technology. When Harry threw the clubs in the lake, Goldballs'n Sak got a good laugh watching it. Seeing what he did next for preparing to host the lunch was a blast.

Harry was still outraged over Han's arrogance and from being denied a mortgage modification. Anger management was what he really needed, but the next best thing would do, which was a pedicure and butt waxing. He didn't want to hear complaints about his hairy ass from the Wall Street Elite. While leaving the Han Jahb Capitol Spa, he saw the Birds of Prey Bipartisan Gift Shop and had a drunken idea. He needed a wet suit for the awards lunch and was surprised at the great selection. The tailor cut out the ass section to fully show the goods. Harry thought he was now prepared for the most prestigious and privileged power lunch in Washington, DC.

The Wall Street Annual Corporate Welfare Extortion Awards Luncheon was to honor business leaders who profited the most from government largesse. This event was founded after Super Congress passed the $700 billion TARP program. The TARP (Troubled-Ass Reckless Politicians) program was focused on providing welfare to companies that had destroyed the world's financial system. It was to bail out banks, insurance companies, auto companies, and any other company deemed "Too Big to Fail." The program is considered a success because most has now been paid back. Because there is still plenty of corporate welfare, the lunch continued. Everybody considered it fun to see who stole the most legally each year. It was very informal and friendly because everybody was not in jail and was getting away with legally stealing by buying politicians.

"This afternoon, we get to recognize two corporations that have received billions of dollars in government assistance," Harry began. "These companies are redefining greatness. Their excellence is unsurpassed. They make us question whether capitalism still exists. It is hard to believe that in this day and age, corporations depend on our government to make their record profits.

"As you know, I am taking Dick Melong's place today. He wanted me to mention something he is working on. As all of you know, we are exempt from insider trading laws. Profiting from using non-public information to buy and sell stock makes all of you millions. I am working on legislation to change this because it is unethical by betraying the public trust.

"I could use a tequila shot and another Seven-inch Ramrod, please." This was speedily brought to Harry, and he downed the shot.

"Dick Melong wanted me to assure you that he has a work-around for my legislation. He has had a phone app created that provides deadlines for when to buy and sell stocks based on all our non-public information. It is called the Dumb Ass Stock List. It gives the stock deadline to buy and sell before the public reacts to what we already know.

"He wanted me to give you an example of how it will work. After President OBaby Domay's State of the Union Speech, the stocks of the two companies we are recognizing today will be crushed. You must sell these stocks by the speech or you are a dumb ass as seen on the list. After the speech, good luck having a retirement worth anything if you do not follow the list.

"Now, I need to mention that I got denied my Han Jahb Loan Modification. You will notice that I am wearing a wet suit. This is because I am trying to survive my underwater mortgage. Please notice that I cut out the ass. I have had it waxed because I don't want any complaints." Harry turned around and showed his naked ass. The crowd laughed because they knew how the system worked.

Harry continued, "Yes, I had to get my ass waxed to fast track my loan modification! I am the last one to find out." The crowd laughed again.

"I am not as rich as all of you. I wasn't asking for any corporate welfare. I'm not above the law like all of you. It is great to be here. There are a few things I feel must be said about your total disregard for the blind consent that the American people have provided to be completely used and manipulated for your financial gain.

"OK. I could use another drink! Please make it a Long Island Iced Tea with another shot," he said, slurring as he looked down at his notes and exhaled loudly into the microphone.

"Americans are enraged that corporate welfare bailed the arrogant Wall Street elite. Wall Street made sure our government did nothing to help the middle class. Americans are becoming disenchanted about being used for political and financial gain. Nothing is being done to stop the corporate welfare because you own Super Congress World. Not only could you steal from the American people, but they will even help you recover. There was no safety net for the American middle class. They were left with depleted savings, no retirement, tax bills, home equity destruction, unaffordable health care, credit card limit cuts, vehicle repossession, foreclosure, home short sales, bankruptcy, and outrageously expensive cable and Internet bills.

"Now, I'm only getting started here. As a member of Super Congress World, I need to vent about our flagrant abuse of power."

The crowd looked at each other smiling because they enjoyed seeing the drunk Financial Services Committee Chairman speaking his mind openly.

HAMMER FUC PLAN

- Fighting to stay middle class
- Unequal treatment
- Crushing amounts of debt

Harry continued, "Fighting to stay middle class has become more difficult with our government ignoring the people. Our incompetence, greed, and ineptitude have destroyed the wealth of the middle class. It is a shame to say, but we did not protect and preserve their way of life. Their sudden destruction blinded us with denial. This denial was used to fool us into thinking things were getting better. The middle class did one thing wrong. They put their trust in self-serving, sellout politicians who caused their way of life to be stolen. It was the greatest wealth displacement in the history of humankind. All of you, the arrogant Wall Street elite, now have that wealth."

Harry paused and braced himself on the podium because he was slurring his words and having trouble standing in the cold wet suit he was sweating in.

Harry slurred, "If you are a stupid politician, whom do you destroy first? When the market was tanking, Baby Boomers sold their retirement investments at the bottom to protect their nest egg during the bust of October 2008. These Boomers won't be able to retire. Who cares about retirement when only survival matters? Others will get a part-time job to get by or cut back on living expenses—if this is still possible. Many of their savings have been depleted.

"I could us another Long Island because I am just getting warmed up. Thanks."

Sweat was now causing Harry to wipe his forehead. He wanted to take the hot wet suit off.

Harry said, "Unequal treatment is now a standard practice of our government. Our government allows the rich and well connected to legally steal without going to jail. Our government has failed the non-millionaires. Unaffordable promises have bought votes. The costs of this were left to the broke middle class to pay. Politicians just pretend to listen and care about them. I am sorry for giving their money to the rich and corporations through tax cuts, cash subsidies, free loans, and special regulations.

"Excuse me a minute. This is nothing all of you haven't seen before." Harry had had enough. He stripped the wet suit off and stood naked at the podium. "All of you have seen this. Where was I? OK?" said Harry.

The crowd looked shocked, and many were laughing. They had all heard about the golf club settlement earlier and wanted to see his drunken ass break down even more.

Harry continued, "The people can't afford to hire high-priced lobbyists to buy favors. They are just controlled and manipulated into believing lies. The truth remains hidden and elusive. The only real thing is that we spend more and get less as our income shrinks with all the Wall Street schemes. One of these schemes is how banks get zero-interest loans, while we get impossible loan requirements and no help for properties that are underwater. The well connected get help, and working families get nothing.

"Crushing amounts of debt are destroying our economy. Our nation is going bankrupt, and we remain frozen in inaction. The accumulation of debt is now a catastrophe and a major national security issue. We have no cash to shelter us from our enemies or the damage from the natural disasters of hurricanes, tornadoes, tsunamis, or earthquakes. It's a disgrace that our leaders are not held accountable. Our sad and worthless display of leadership undermines our ability to make necessary changes. Our nation has to borrow money to support our addiction to the spending that is destroying this country.

"Who controls the global financial system? Enigmatic corporations control our interconnected global financial system. These corporations are so large and complex that regulation and oversight is impossible with sellout politicians.

"One of the companies that we will recognize tonight is a banking enigma and the other is an insurance enigma. Both of these companies do the same thing. We just say one is banking and the other is insurance. Both specialize in providing legal stealing services, hedge fund scams, fraud settlement consulting, insider trading accounts, tax avoidance strategies, financial bubble consulting, and placement services for politicians. These two companies have mastered world dominance by owning our government. Some of us are great at helping our fellow Americans, and some are great at stealing from them. We are here to recognize those great at stealing.

Harry downed his drink and shifted his weight to stay up. "Ready for another. Enigma corporations have not been ignored during this time of great hardship for many Americans. The billions in profits they are earning make it easier to ignore the real people who need help in our country. We gave a hand out and hand up to make sure corporations and the rich survive our economic crises without hardship. Now that we are broke, nothing will be done to help American families.

"Our financial system collapse was done on two fronts. The banks and insurance collapse was to defraud Americans and our government in October 2008. The two companies we are recognizing today conspired together to profit from the destruction of our financial markets. We are here to recognize the leaders of Steptin Schibt Bank and the Bad Insurance Group. I would like to introduce the CEO of Steptin Schibt Bank, Han Jahb. These companies are working hard at getting your ass—that's Americans' Small Savings."

It was 12:30 p.m., and the food was now being brought out. Everybody was drinking too much and having a blast watching Harry go to pieces.

Han Jahb shook his hand at the podium. "Many thanks to all of you. I have to tell you that I am tired of hearing about how Steptin Schibt Bank did not give Harry Brokass a loan modification," he said. "We don't give loan mods because of all the fraudulent mortgages and worthless securities we sold the American people and pension funds. You cannot expect us to modify our own fraud mortgage. This is bad business. We deny all loan mods.

"I would like to take a moment to explain what makes us successful. Your zero-interest loans, tax loopholes, other favors, and ineptitude provided us with another record year. I feel all those campaign contributions and jobs to the well connected are paying off."

Harry looked perplexed. He had put his wet suit back on and was drinking water because of the dehydration.

"Our business has been transformed by the Goldballs'n Sak FUC Plan. This involves fraudulent financial innovation, unquestioned power and arrogance, and corrupt government.

GOLDBALLS'N SAK FUC PLAN

- Fraudulent financial innovations
- Unquestioned power and arrogance
- Corrupt government

"Fraudulent financial innovations are the foundation of our banking industry and security markets. Steptin Schibt Bank is the best in class for financial innovation, whether it is legal or not. We are leaders in the financial industry. Whether it is real estate, insurance, or commodities markets, Steptin Schibt is specialized at making up lies to profit from markets going up and down. For years, Steptin Schibt Bank made huge profits by making the investing public,

401(K) plans, mutual funds, and pension funds believe they were buying high-rated securities. We sold them worthless securities. The damage to the American public, clients, or governments does not matter to us. We only care about making money.

"All of us at Steptin Schibt Bank want to thank you for the zero-interest loans. We take this money to invest in our stock market or overseas investments. We make highly speculative investments with your money. This is risk-free for us, but your ass is on the line. Many of our competitors have gone out of business. Those of us who are left are making billions. Without your corporate welfare, we would not be making record profits. We made so much from stealing from the American people that is hard to believe your generosity in helping us to make even more from stealing from you again. All I need to do is play golf at Super Congress World.

"Unquestioned power and arrogance are cornerstones to great banking. Being on government assistance doesn't mean you are poor. The poor just give it a bad name. We are always looking for new talent. Making millions a year is easy. Staying out of jail can be tricky. It is not difficult, is it, to make up lies and more lies to inform investors. We are one of the largest and most prestigious banks in the world. What we say is the truth. Our smart attorneys and MBAs are needed to keep track of our web of lies and investment schemes.

"Sometimes we invest our clients' money and then bet their investment will lose value. Nobody would question a bank with our reputation and talented crooks and politicians working for us. Our reputation proves that we are never wrong.

"Corrupt government is needed to create worthless securities and to keep us out of jail. Getting away with the oldest trick in the book took genius. Inept, sellout, and lazy politicians are perfect for hands-off, no-enforcement government. Not enforcing existing laws makes stealing legal. Certainly, the most powerful country on earth would have regulators who could figure this out.

"Let me assure you that our government condones Steptin Schibt's business practices. This includes the practice of secret lending, shadow banking, and predatory loans. We appreciate government officials' hands-off approach. They ignored all the red flags and informants. They made it legal to steal and condoned how we do business. I want to play golf with them because they keep me out of jail.

If you are a genius and you're going to steal from investors, you make it legal. Politicians wanting to look as if they were helping businesses were more than willing to lend us a helping hand. We have made billions by receiving government assistance. Somebody has to win here, and we are above the laws you created. We will get what we want with or without you. None of us have gone to jail. We are your new reality. We own your government and are above the law. We will remember your gratitude and are touched. Thank you," said Han Jahb.

Harry took the podium. "After hearing all that, I'm ready for a junket and freebies." The crowd laughed.

"Where are my notes? OK. Hear we go again. The next business leaders take no introduction. Their made-up achievements are unforgettable. They are now helping our country by working for one of the most despised corporations in history. They are joint CEOs of the Bad Insurance Group. They are the only ones who can get the job done. Please welcome Butch and Chainsaw."

Butch and Chainsaw went up to the podium.

"Thank ya," said Butch.

"It's great to be here," Chainsaw added.

"It is great to be around friends where I can speak openly. Harry is certainly doing this," Butch said as the crowd roared in laughter.

Butch continued, "The rewarding extortion provisions in the Dick Melong Wall Street Reform and Rewarding Extortion legislation is the basis for growth in our industry. All of us know insurance is extortion. Our insurance business is founded on solid extortion principles that have built and rebuilt Wall Street. Growing our business is easy with the government's business-friendly extortion laws.

"We appreciate taxpayers' paying our business losses for the worthless securities we insured. Please look at us like a casino because this was a jackpot for us. We risk nothing with your bailout loans, so expect more losses as we continue to gamble with your money. Thanks for another great year."

Chainsaw said, "Our enhanced insurance techniques are getting great results at defrauding our clients. Look at how we insured worthless securities and helped Steptin Schibt Bank survive. We're willing to insure a turd being flushed down the toilet. This is just what we did to Americans' home values. Butch and I were made for the insurance business. Thank you all."

The audience applauded, shaking their heads.

"It's good to hear that both of these companies are experiencing solid growth on corporate welfare," Harry said, retaking the podium. "Our legislation is working. The larger question is if we can help working families. It is time for more shared responsibilities in such a huge displacement of wealth. For all of you, I realize you do not think our system is broken. You own Super Congress World, and you're winning," Harry abruptly stated.

The audience stood up and applauded enthusiastically as Harry walked out, shaking hands. They liked seeing a good fight. Harry went directly to the bar: Going to Rehab.

I was already there when he arrived and said, "Everybody loved your speech."

Harry said, "Wow. I get to meet the man who destroyed my life and the world financial system. Without you, I would not have been motivated to hold elected office."

"Let me get you a Seven-inch Ramrod," I said.

"Thanks," said Harry smirking. "I know you are behind all this."

"You have a nice ass. Getting it waxed will assure you of the loan mod because it looks so damn good," I said.

"You built Wall Street!" shouted Harry loudly. "There has to be more than just crooks!"

"You were brutally honest. Do you think it will accomplish anything?" I said.

"No, but it was good to vent. At this point, only the voters will decide," said Harry.

I said, "The voters work for me. Our lies and deception will keep the illusion of democracy going."

Day 5: Wall Street Survival Guide on How to Screw Your Shareholders, Customers, and All Taxpayers by Buying Politicians to Get Rich by Goldballs'n Sak and Han Jahb

On Wednesday, January 18, 2012, Han and I were going to speak at the 2011 Steptin Schibt Annual Shareholder Meeting. We were going to open the event at nine a.m. After partying late into the night with key company executives, it might not have been the best idea.

"Are you up for this? We have not even recovered from last night," I said to Han Jahb.

"My head hurts. We only have short statements to make. This will be fine," said Han as he walked to the podium.

"Great to see all of you again," he began. "I have to share with you about my golf outing yesterday with Harry Brokass. He unsuccessfully attempted to qualify for our loan modification. I cannot stop laughing over how upset and outraged he was over being denied. I tried to calm him down by letting him know we deny everybody. If this was not bad enough, I also told him his male boobs were ruining his golf swing. This did not go over too well because he thought I was just making fun of him. I hurt from laughing."

Han took a moment to collect himself. "Steptin Schibt Bank has had another excellent year. As you know, our stock has not increased in value. This is because of the huge salaries and bonuses paid to our executives and employees. I can assure you that this will not change, so you might want to consider selling your Steptin Schibt Bank shares. You can always fire me for this. Good luck trying to find someone who understands our complicated and convoluted business." Han looked at the bartender and raised his empty glass for another round.

"Our company is stuffed with former politicians with law degrees who keep us out of jail and make us money. Not only do we not care about our shareholders, we do not care about our customers, either. In the coming year, our focus will remain on increasing employee wealth."

"The former chairman of our board, Goldballs'n Sak, is running for president of the United States. As all of you know, I replaced him as CEO in 2007. His innovative leadership took legal stealing and paying settlements to unconscionable heights. We are fortunate for him to join us today to explain how our favorable regulations are going to help our business. Please welcome the next president of the United States— Goldballs'n Sak," said Han as he shook hands and left the podium.

"It is great to be here today. Thank you," I said as the crowd stood applauded enthusiastically. "To end the threat of meaningful financial regulations or enforcement, we need to make sure I become president." They clapped while sitting down. I downed my drink and continued, "Wall Street faces the threat of ridiculous regulations that have nothing to do with how we do business. I will protect the Dick Melong Wall Street Reform and Rewarding Extortion Act. Its impact on your business is what I will be covering today.

"When this reform was being created, Wall Street asked for everything, hoping to get something to exploit. To everybody's surprise, everything on the list was put into the bill. Because of budget constraints,

Congress even assured us that enforcement would be lenient.

"This reform will do much to help our business. This legislation was designed to protect the two things we hold most dear: creating worthless securities and profiting from inside information. Wall Street is designing innovative ways to exploit this reform for enormous profits.

"What business model will help you to adapt to these positive regulatory changes? Simply put: fictitious high-risk investments, undeterminable legal liabilities, and crash and burn. This is based on the Grab-Your-Ankles FUC Plan.

GRAB-YOUR-ANKLES FUC PLAN

- Fictitious high-risk investments
- Undeterminable legal liabilities
- Crash and burn

"A fictitious high-risk investment takes innovation. Selling worthless securities is the oldest scam in the world. Business expansion from easy credit, bank fraud, and lack of oversight caused a global financial meltdown or the Great Depression II. Today our government gives Steptin Schibt Bank corporate welfare that includes interest-free loans, a lack of regulation, and tax-free benefits. Let me assure you that when I become president, this will not change.

"Undeterminable legal liabilities will be an ongoing issue because our government will continue to allow you to do whatever you want, regardless of the law. Profits will be questionable and illusionary until large settlements are paid. When you get caught, the former politicians who work for Steptin Schibt will be expected to negotiate a favorable settlement to protect you from the parties we've schemed. Unethical practices are rewarded and encouraged. Regulations are a good thing as long as they are not enforced and the public believes they are being protected. Your money is safer in Las Vegas than in a bank.

"Finally, crash and burn. This is for shareholders, customers, and taxpayers. This is the result that we can expect when former politicians work for you in and out of office. If nobody goes to jail for selling worthless securities, only a catastrophic outcome can be expected. Without political support, you would be in jail, dead, or selling drugs. Credit is the ultimate drug of mass destruction. No matter how smart investors think they are, they will lose. Wall Streets tricks and schemes will get your money because the house always wins."

"I have to say thank you for allowing me to be here today. You know I will look after your interests." The crowd stood up and clapped while Han shook hands with me at the podium.

"Thank you for coming today," Han said as I sat down in the front row. "We have to put up with crooks in elected office because we have to keep crooks in our own offices around the world. Our highly talented employees need to appear to be creating legitimate deals done in our complex global world. Crooks helping crooks is what we must do to maintain growth and expand into new markets that appear to be legitimate. Our executives are vigilant in adjusting to constantly changing political connections."

Han was served another drink as he braced himself against the podium.

"What will we do to ensure enormous profits and enough cash to pay legal settlements? Being a fee-collection machine, using unpredictable market manipulation, and providing consulting services will accomplish this. This is referred to as the Giving-The-Shaft FUC Plan.

GIVING-THE-SHAFT FUC PLAN

- Fee-collection machine
- Unpredictable market manipulation
- Consulting services

"Our banks are fee-collecting machines. We charge for everything. With our government not guaranteeing loans, risky lending would not be possible. Our biggest fear is that debt slaves will pay down credit card debt, car loans, student loans, or mortgages.

"Another thing: Unpredictable market manipulation trading with high volatility provides enormously profitable opportunities. One of the most established investment strategies is High-Frequency Trading. Under HFT, a transaction's life may be less than a second. It's ironic: Wall Street tells people to buy for the long-term when we are in and out of a stock or option in less than a second. Financial experts tell everybody to diversify and not to sell for years when one hour is long-term for us. We are masters at making money if the market goes up or down, regardless of our clients' or shareholders' interests. We recommend investments to customers and investors because we are going to do the exact opposite of what we say.

"Our computer engineers and software developers have created exciting pioneering technology for us to exploit this year," Han paused and downed his drink. "I haven't been this excited about anything since that $20,000-an-hour whore I had last night." He paused, laughing. "Sorry, that is just the cocaine talking. You are going to love this!"

The crowd just looked at each other, perplexed. This was when I realized that we should have cancelled the speech.

"Our cutting-edge technology will allow us to back the bus up on anybody in our way. The latest supercomputers have allowed us to create a totally new investment strategy called Super Highly Automated Frequency Technology. SHAFT will give us the competitive advantage to steam roll over all of our competition and the investing public. We're going to SHAFT everything we can. We can specialize in exploiting oil markets with SHAFT trading speculation. When you fill up your gas tank, rest assured we are giving you the SHAFT. When you see your investment account decreasing more and more, you are getting the SHAFT. The SHAFT is redefining our business.

SHAFT

- Super
- Highly
- Automated
- Frequency
- Technology

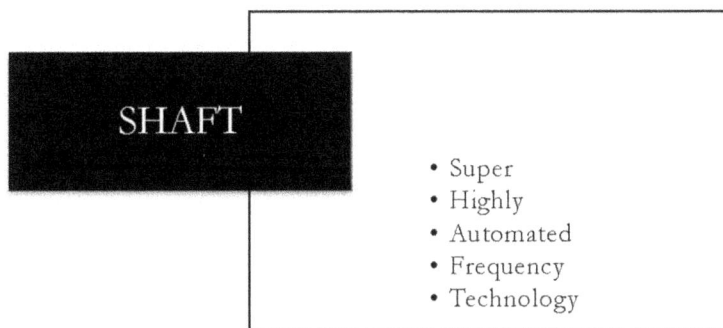

"SHAFT trading is very sensitive, so we have to protect it with misinformation because information controls our investment markets and account balances. Our large and expensive advertising buys are in high demand from media companies. They will be silenced into saying nothing negative about us. Our media markets will be flooded with independent stories on the importance of long-term diversified retirement planning to keep the sheep giving us their retirement. Our supercomputers SHAFT trade about one million transactions a day. Nobody can hide from SHAFT trading.

"This technology is so new that it is unregulated. Our politicians cannot keep up with our innovations. Our SHAFT trading has ended the concept of buy and hold, but don't tell anybody. Nobody can retire as long as we can SHAFT them.

"Finally, our consulting services are mined for insider information. This is our greatest source of market manipulation and insider trading opportunities. When it comes to selling and insuring worthless securities, shadow financing, secret government lending, blackmail projects, tax avoidance services, kickbacks and side dealing on infrastructure building, contract guarantees on federal acquisition budgets, or oil extortion strategies, we provide the finest consulting services in the world. Many of these are new projects that are kept confidential. Because of our expansive, politically connected client base, we are in a strategic position to profit from sensitive insider information that only the well connected can misuse.

"In the coming year, you shareholders will be out of luck again. Figuring out how to circumvent extra regulations and implement SHAFT technology will create many opportunities for employees to cash in this year. This extra work will mean bigger bonuses that will decrease shareholder value.

"We can thank politicians in and out of office for helping us legally steal. They saved us, so that we can legally steal again. Let me assure you that we provide full disclosure on our fraudulent securities and unethical practices to keep the stealing legal. Uninformed, sellout, and complacent politicians protect us.

"It was great to be here today. Thank you."

Day 6: How to Get Elected With a Double Down on Corrupt Leadership and Locking Americans or Non-millionaire Voter Sheep out of the Voting Booth by Dick Melong

Harry Brokass' breakdown and the shareholder meeting were bothering me until I realized what I should have noticed sooner. It was around two a.m. on Friday, my favorite golfing day, January 20, 2012, at the Dick Melong Capitol Bathhouse when I realized what I had caused.

The rain showers next to the 'Going To Rehab' bar were hot and steaming up. The special interests I was with were the hottest guys I had ever seen. After too many house specials, everything seemed to melt away when I realized what I had done. It was obvious when I looked back. My closest friends were being destroyed by the truth. My vodka was a truth serum. The truth was not something that Washington DC could handle. Everything I had worked my entire life for was unraveling. Surprisingly, I was the happiest I had ever been. One thing was clear to me: there was no way I was going to give up my excessive vodka drinking or Seven-inch Ramrods.

I slept that night at the Steptin Schibt spa meeting room. I sent Dick Melong a text that I could not attend his training seminar, which was at ten a.m. Dick called me at nine a.m. and insisted that I go. He assured me that it would not be like his last one and that it was important for my election. During our conversation, I realized that he was going to say the truth again, so I agreed to go. After a lot of coffee and some vodka, I went upstairs to a large meeting room at the Scott Free Capitol Bar.

Dick saw me arrive a few minutes after ten a.m. and got started. "Thank you for coming to my seminar: How To Get Elected With a Double Down on Corrupt Leadership and Locking Americans or Non-millionaire Voter Sheep Out of the Voting Booth. You are probably asking yourself: What does corrupt leadership have to do with shutting voters out of the voting box? We do not do anything; so to get elected, we have to lock out anybody who will not vote for us.

Voter sheep are too stupid to figure this out. Denying one of our most cherished privileges is true corruption. You decide when to leave office and not the sheep.

"What is corrupt leadership? I optimize corrupt leadership."

At this point, all I could think was how Dick had trapped these officials into this one. There was nothing I could do but order a double.

"The skills I am covering are applicable to strong leadership, even if you have no competence or talent. I provide real, solid corrupt business and political leadership. This seminar will focus on two points: corrupt leadership and campaign reform.

"It would be good if I start by explaining my background. When I built my health insurance company, I committed billions in fraud insurance billings. My company paid the largest Medicare fraud fine of all time, $3 billion. Overbilling on prescriptions, procedures not performed, fake doctor visits, unneeded medical equipment—you name it, they were all standard practice. I know how to build a business and get things done. To hide from the law, I sought elected office over twenty years ago.

"How does great legislation help you build a business to create jobs in these difficult economic times? In the Dick Melong Wall Street Reform and Rewarding Extortion Act, I know how to profit from rewarding extortion. I am proud to say this legislation was going nowhere unless I got my rewarding extortion provisions.

"Creating sound insurance extortion legislation is important to cashing in when I am out of office. When you are in office, you need to plan how to get rich quick when you are out of office. That's why I helped write the Wall Street reform bill. Insurance is extortion. When I built my health insurance company, we legally stole billions. You do not see me in jail because I pleaded the Fifth Amendment. Insurance is the perfect business when you buy politicians in and out of office to write the laws and regulations that reward extortion.

"What are the sound fundamentals of insurance extortion that business-friendly legislation must support? This involves the Insurance Extortion FUC Plan: forced compliance, unaffordable fees and premiums, and costs spiraling out of control.

INSURANCE EXTORTION FUC PLAN

- Forced compliance
- Unaffordable fees and premiums
- Costs spiraling out of control

"Forced compliance allows insurance companies to extort money. Want to live? Health insurance might help with some of your costs to prevent bankruptcy. Want to drive a car? Auto insurance is required. Have a mortgage? Homeowner's insurance is required. Want to rent an apartment? Renter's insurance may be required. This lack of choice amounts to extortion.

"Unaffordable fees and premiums have to be paid. Working to just pay health insurance costs is inexcusable. Some Americans even have to choose low-paying jobs just to have insurance coverage. Health insurance for families has become unaffordable. You must pay or suffer and die. Health insurance reform is going to subsidize unaffordable premiums. This will help us to extort more. Businesses and individuals are maxed out. Scamming our government into paying health insurance subsidies offers us a gold mine.

"Costs spiraling out of control cause all of us to pay more and get less. Nobody is doing anything to control costs, so insurance companies can dictate costs, which is extortion. Businesses need a healthy work force, so many pay a portion of their employees' health insurance cost. Individuals pay for doctor visits, deductibles, and in- and out-of-network scams as part of the extortion. We had many exclusions in our insurance policies to prevent paying claims because we do not want our clients to extort from us. You pay no matter what, with or without insurance.

"The Bad Insurance Group eventually bought my overvalued medical company twenty years ago. Goldballs'n Sak at Steptin Schibt Bank arranged the deal, which burned BIG bad. In the end, they financed my campaign for me to be here today. Goldballs'n Sak and I have remained close over the years. Both of us share a love for vodka and golf.

"Does anybody have any questions?"

He had to ask, I thought as I ordered another double.

"What do you think we can do to cut Ponzi scheme entitlement programs?" asked a newly elected congressman.

Dick downed his drink and said, "Have you ever had sex in a car when the windows get steamed up and a cop shines his flashlight at you? Then you find yourself in jail and get anally raped? This is what will happen if you mess with entitlements.

"Economists have a term for this. It is called dumpster planning. When you cut entitlements, Americans will end up living naked in dumpsters.

Older Americans will get out of that dumpster, put underwear on, and kick your ass."

If that wasn't enough, we got another question.

"Why can't we get rid of a lot of needless government agencies?" asked a senator while Dick was served another drink.

"This is definitely a concern of our party. Have you ever had sex and had the condom break? Then your wife finds out when the housekeeper has the baby and puts a restraining order on you." Dick finished his drink. "My point here is that politicians who want to eliminate needed agencies should have restraining orders put on them until they are voted out of office. You ungrateful millionaires will need to learn the history of the gifts that have been provided to us.

"Sometimes government agencies kill for businesses to profit. When I built my medical business, our government approved fraudulent and defective drugs that did not work and actually harmed the public. There were diabetes, arthritis, and anti-cholesterol drugs that caused heart attacks and strokes. These drugs were killing the patients I needed to use for my fraudulent Medicare and Medicaid billings.

"Government agencies are also important to paying business expenses. Shifting expenses from business to government is our responsibility as politicians. This is how we get rich when we are out of office. Wall Street will facilitate nationalizing business losses. Nothing increases profits like having somebody else paying. Health insurance is a great example. Exploding health costs are hurting business profits, so getting government to pay will increase business profits and get us a job once we leave office. Another example is worthless securities. The claims get paid by our government, which ends up owning them. The middle class gets no help because those of us in power provide no help to them. Spend and spend more to buy votes with lies is all that counts. It is an injustice to the American people that nobody is going to jail.

"What is corrupt leadership? My entire business and political career are based on corruption. My Dick Melong Wall Street Reform and Rewarding Extortion Act allows Wall Street to actually legally sell worthless securities and exploit insider information. Yes, Wall Street will always do this because they own Super Congress World, and it does not matter who is in or out of office. Because of this, working class families have been exploited and many lives have been destroyed. Any Wall Street reform that might protect and preserve American families will eventually be dismantled or not enforced. Lack of commitment from all parties and sellout politicians will always make the system flawed. Money and power will always make us corrupt. Just the appearance of reform is needed.

"To keep America strong, I am sponsoring landmark legislation for campaign reform that will make it easier for us to stay in office. All of us know that sellout, lying politicians rule our country. Say anything and do nothing is how you get elected. The Dick Melong Overpromise and Underdeliver Campaign Reform Act holds officials to certain standards. This act, which I am quite proud of, mandates compliance to the standards of the Double Down Election FUC Plan of foolish blockade leadership, unconscionable voter lockout, and crazy lies to get elected or remain in office.

DOUBLE DOWN ELECTION FUC PLAN

- Foolish blockade leadership
- Unconscionable voter lockout
- Crazy lies

"Foolish blockade leadership involves blaming the other party and doing nothing to protect American families. We just collect our paycheck on do nothing at our part-time golfing jobs.

"Unconscionable voter lockouts need to filter out voter sheep who will not vote for us. This is an absolute disgrace to our party and country. One sure way to tell corrupt politicians is whether they lock Americans out of the voting booth. The submissive voter sheep will do what we have trained them for, even if this training is based on lies.

"Finally, crazy lies will keep us in office. People will actually believe the garbage we say. Lies to maintain the illusion of safety and security are another hallmark of fake leadership. The best example is how the unemployment rate is a lie to manipulate public opinion. A rule of thumb is that actual rate of unemployment is twice what they report. If we say it is 9 percent, in reality it is around 18 percent. This is because the calculation does not include the people who stopped looking and those who are underemployed. The employment-to-population ratio is the actual wake-up call here. Ignore the unemployment rate lie, which is just intended to manipulate public attention and the debate.

"Let's not forget that real leaders make sure somebody else pays. Deficit spending is just to buy votes without raising taxes or cutting expenses. Avoid real action at all costs and forget about shared sacrifice. Balanced approaches will not work.

"My legislation is the biggest crazy lie of all. Middle-class Americans get ignored. Only business is protected and preserved. Higher education has become unaffordable. Real estate is in meltdown. Our government has become a bank. Our jobs crisis has caused great hardship. Rebuilding your life on lower-paying full- or part-time jobs is impossible. The blind consent and silent obedience of voter sheep is causing their own demise.

"Any questions?"

No way. I can't believe he is doing this again, I thought while finishing my double.

"Is anybody in Super Congress World not corrupt?" said somebody I had never seen before.

Dick took a sip of his drink and said, "Do I look as if I enjoy wearing women's lingerie, especially nylons with thong underwear? Harry Brokass is honest, but he cannot even get a loan modification playing by the rules."

I was sitting in shock listening to all of this. The conflict between winning my campaign with lies or destroying my life with the truth was causing me to drink even more as I ordered another double.

Another bitch asked, "You do a lot of complaining. What real solutions do you have?"

Dick thought as he downed his drink and motioned for another. He said, "Have you ever shaved your private parts and accidently cut yourself? Then you learn how painful it is taking the bandage off. It would have hurt even worse if I hadn't shaved my balls. I did this yesterday, and it hurts like a son of a bitch because I also had an allergic reaction to the latex or the bandage glue."

"My point here is that sometimes the solution becomes the problem. The solution that we offer the American public for everything is RAGE. RAGE will wake them up. How do we define RAGE? RAGE stands for **R**oot for failure, **A**ttack the other party for all failure, **G**ridlock at all costs, and **E**asy election win. People will rise up in RAGE.

He took a deep breath and said, "I do have a RAGE FUC Plan. This involves Frustrated voters, Urgent action, and Continued prosperity. Frustrated voters are suffering from the posttraumatic stress syndrome of having their way of life stolen by our FUC Plans. Urgent action is needed, but all we deliver on is blaming the other party. Continued prosperity for the rich and neglecting non-millionaire American families is the result of everything we do.

"When voters do not believe us, what should we do?" asked another bitch.

"Really, you have not figured that out? Have you ever slept with a $10,000-an-hour prostitute and wondered if it was worth it? We are the prostitutes, you dumb-ass! Do you think you are here for free? This is Super Congress World. It is a whorehouse. You need to wake up even more than the voter sheep. The only difference between a whore and us is that we don't have the cash on the nightstand when we leave. Any more questions?"

"How can we stay in office with all this corruption?" asked some bitch.

"Great question!" Dick paused while downing his drink. "Have you ever woken up naked in a dumpster with a pacifier in your mouth and your thumb up your ass?"

Many smiled while shaking their heads and were shocked that he had really lost it.

Dick said, "This is where you belong. You can sleep well because voters have not figured this out. Thank you."

Day 7: State of the Union Address: Because I Am No Longer Immobilized from the Demise of My Magical Unicorn, We Can Recover from the Post-Traumatic Stress Syndrome Caused by Wall Street Stealing Home Equity, Retirement, and Jobs, or Let's Just Say Everything You Worked Your Entire Life For.

On Tuesday, January 24, 2012, I was finishing a drink in a bar called 'The Shovel' at the Scott Free Capitol Bar. It had a forty-foot LED screen. Many special interests and lobbyists were present. My campaign manager came to give me an update.

"We can meet with Dick tomorrow at seven a.m. to go over our reaction," said Wrecking Balls.

"Good," I said. "I read the speech, and he slams us pretty badly."

"Yes, he is trying to destroy Wall Street," said Wrecking Balls. "I heard a rumor that OBaby is addicted to your vodka. Apparently, some incident occurred last Sunday when he got trashed watching football at the White House.

"Try to find out more. This would mean my vodka will win me the election," I said and ordered a double for each of us.

President OBaby Domay began the speech before we started watching, "If there is one thing I have to do, it's to get American families out of this financial crisis. Many of our fellow Americans are going through great hardships. Unemployment is still our major challenge. Bankruptcies and foreclosures are too widespread. When I came into office, our world financial system was in meltdown.

"All of us know our government is dysfunctional. The circus of fucking Congress must cease. We must speak openly about being cluster fucked by Wall Street psychopaths."

I burst into laughter. My vodka had struck again. He trashed the speech from what we were given.

OBaby went on as everybody looked shocked, "Politicians just say what you want to hear, and Americans are disillusioned by the tricks and scams of sellout politicians. You must be tired of hearing the same things with no meaningful action.

"The altered reality of Congress gone wild must end. The finger-pointing must end. It makes it look as if nothing is getting done. Many politicians will always be self-serving assholes who know how to manipulate the masses for their own gain. Legalized extortion starts with politicians. They receive campaign money and employment after holding office. The incompetence and constant blaming keeps this country in a quagmire with no leadership. The end result is that American families are ignored.

"Avoiding discussing issues with the public prevents politicians from dealing with real concerns. Rampant unemployment, which happened because of incompetent leadership, is destroying our country. Fucking Congress gets what it wants, and American families suffer. You give support to the government, and we repay you by outsourcing jobs to Asia and with low-paying jobs, reduced benefits, and a lack of job security.

"Fucking Congress does not work. This is why I am going directly to you, the American people. You are demanding action from all political parties. Getting results is what you elected me for. Our politics must step up to meet our challenges. Chains of debt are hindering change and growth. You need access to cash to rebuild your life. We need to be respectful and stop wasting and neglecting your lives.

"Consumer demand must drive us to economic growth in creating jobs. Now is the time to take new, bold initiatives. Consumer spending needs to increase to improve our future. This will drive the expansion for growth in demand and supply for goods and services. We will focus on tax cuts, spending cuts, and simplified sensible regulation. Our hard work will achieve great things. We are now at a turning point and must make some crucial changes.

"Condemning future generations to debt has become acceptable. We grow our way out of crises by causing crises. Our country has become the world's largest debtor nation. It is hard to believe that people actually vote for politicians. We tell you what you want to hear and then provide giant corporations with huge profits.

"We must focus on a debt reduction plan. We are broke! We have been in denial of this for too long. With a debt reduction plan, all of us will need to make sacrifices. It must be noted that politicians like Dick Melong have caused us to be topped out on our debt limit and have our credit rating cut. Too much free cash has gone to banks and large corporations. Bailing out banks was expected to help you. Help was to trickle down to you. Let me be clear, this trickle down economics is bullshit. We all know, these motherfuckers fucked us over. We are going to cut them off and use this money to help you more directly.

"What works for Wall Street will work for Main Street. I am not saying that Main Street needs $10,000-an-hour prostitutes and illegal drugs. Wall Street owns fucking Congress. When politicians say we will have an industry self-regulate, you are going to get fucked. A great example of this is Super Highly Automated Frequency Technology or SHAFT. This is completely unregulated. Most Wall Street transactions are now less than a second with SHAFT Trading. This risky unregulated market is going to fuck us. You need our government to serve you, not them.

"Let me be clear, Wall Street will not be supporting me for president. Their profits are larger under my administration in three years then the entire eight years of the last administration. I kept them out of jail to use the stolen money on my campaign. Wall Street benefits from our borrowing for business stimuli, business bailouts, and business tax cuts. With all the profits on corporate welfare, nothing trickles down to American families because trickle down economics is bullshit.

"Many of us have different views. Americans like voting for politicians who do nothing for them. The middle class is being destroyed. Some think we are in a class war. Some think our democracy is becoming a kleptocracy. It is time for the people, who are loosing the war, to wake the fuck up.

"We must also compromise or reach a consensus on spending and taxes. What is right for the people is lost in partisan fighting. We will act to do something that does not involve legally stealing your wealth and destroying the middle class. Let me assure you that politics is all about compromise. We are going to compromise as long as we can help you.

"In order for the American families to recover, the playing field must be leveled. We have a detailed plan with four programs that focus on helping everyone to rebuild their lives. These new initiatives will take commitment and determination to make today better. This is the ZERO Plan, and it's centered around you. It is crucial to our economic survival that you become financially sound. Let me be clear, the ZERO Plan is a real solution and not pretend legislation.

"If it works for Wall Street, it will work for Main Street. It is now time to give the power back to the people—and to give you access to cash. The ZERO Plan was designed to do this. It includes Zero-interest loans, Easy debt refinancing, Requiring a minimum tax on businesses and the wealthy, and One-time retirement withdrawal. This plan will help you recover from the post-traumatic stress syndrome of being fucked by Wall Street.

"First, I propose zero-interest loans will allow you to restructure debt and strengthen your finances. This loan program will vary according to the type of debt. Mortgages and business start-up loans will go as high as $200,000. This loan program is a powerful tool for you to rebuild your life. You will be able to refinance mortgages, student loans, car loans, and credit card debt. Here are the loan terms: These zero-interest loans will gradually ramp up to a 2 percent interest cap over five years. The loans will have up to a twenty-year payback period. Interest will never exceed the 2 percent cap at the five-year mark.

"We already did this for broke banks and large corporations. Banks have done nothing but hand job loan modification programs. We will make them pay for not helping you. They will start paying interest on their interest-free loans. This will help us fund zero-interest loans to you. Only by helping you pay off and restructure your debt can all of us enjoy a more prosperous future.

"Second, there's easy debt refinancing. There will no longer be a requirement to have your ass waxed or for condoms or kneepads. Providing you access to capital is the only way for our economy to grow. The mortgage-refinancing program will be streamlined. All of us know all too well that a complicated process is a way for banks to scam you and hide their fraud and negligence.

"Easy debt refinancing is needed to get you help quicker. Complicated processes create unneeded obstacles. This hinders growth and prevents you from rebuilding your life. Easy debt refinancing will not involve an excessive amount of fees. Wall Street and banks will not be able to use their tricks and schemes to cheat you in this highly simplified process. Having fewer regulations in restructuring debt will cut enforcement costs, as we will make sure all laws and regulations are followed. Regulators will be reviewing this simple process to protect you and our economy. The banks' going back to their old ways will not happen under my watch. Let me be clear, it is time for you to put your kneepads on and fuck them back.

"Third, we will require a minimum income tax for businesses and the wealthy. The tax orgy is over. This even includes oil companies and hedge funds. Taxing is about political favors. As all of you know, many corporations have worked our system to unfair advantages. Some of the well connected do not pay taxes. Decreasing taxes on the wealthy or job creators does not trickle down to American families because trickle down economics is bullshit.

"A line is going to be drawn that business and the wealthy must pay a minimum 30 percent income tax. This tax will be due regardless of your deductions or special treatment. Too many of the rich and wealthy corporations are not paying their fair share because they can buy favorable treatment from fucking Congress. Taxes are just a reelection game to buy votes. We work hard every day, day in and day out. No business should expect to get a free ride from our country.

"Finally, there's the one-time retirement withdrawal. Live today and spend some of your retirement to help our economy. Having access to your retirement money right now will provide you with many opportunities. Go start a business, buy a home with cash, or take a dream vacation. This one-time retirement withdrawal can be used for whatever you decide. Over a two-year period, you will be able to make penalty-free withdrawals from your retirement accounts up to $200,000. It is always a great idea to have savings, but it is just as important to have access to cash to build and change your life.

"The Baby Boom Bust of October 2008 fucked many Americans' retirement accounts and destroyed the very concept of retirement. This program fucks Wall Street over on one of its most lucrative scams. It is time to raid retirement accounts to rebuild our future. We cannot let Wall Street's traps and gimmicks steal your hard-earned money. This one-time retirement withdrawal will allow many Americans to become less chained to debt burdens and worthless Wall Street investments. Many of you may be able to become debt free and have more disposable income. This is what we need for our economy to prosper."

"Another threat also looms over our retirement accounts. Most transactions on Wall Street are less than a second. Many of you do not feel safe with Wall Street's lack of regulation. Wall Street tells you to buy and hold when they make their money in less than a second. As I said earlier, you do not have access to this technology that is called Super Highly Automated Frequency Technology, or SHAFT. Wall Street is giving you the SHAFT, and the ZERO Plan gives you an opportunity to get your money out.

"The ZERO Plan is meant to be simple to make it work for you. The dysfunctional Congress is our main obstacle. Together, we can fuck Congress and get things done that actually help American families.

"The idea that Wall Street always wins can be declared over. All of us can have confidence in our financial system again with the ZERO Plan. These times are redefining our lives and how we perceive financial freedom. Financial freedom means surviving today without getting fucked by Wall Street. Financial planning is not just about retirement. It is about living financially free today.

"We will only realize the great times ahead by helping you right now. Consumer spending rules our economy. Without an increase in consumer spending, our economy will not grow. Zero-interest loans and other creative ideas in the ZERO Plan will jump-start our economy and help get you a paycheck. The ZERO Plan is focused on helping American families and transforming Congress into a body that actually does something that helps people. Helping you improve your life will increase consumer demand, which will drive our economy to new heights. Our only obstacle is fucking Congress.

"The four programs in the ZERO Plan will empower you to rebuild and create the today and tomorrow of your design. All of us can build on our past to make sure that today marks a path to happiness. We have been through a lot together. Strengthening American families will improve our economy and allow us to enjoy life's adventures. We are going to need to be creative and ambitious. Ingenuity and enterprise will help you build a better today and an incredible future. It is your hard work, strength, and determination that will transform our country.

"Our democracy and economy are at a major turning point. Jobs can be created only with a strong consumer, and consumers have been neglected. Entrepreneurs need access to capital to open new businesses. The ZERO Plan has the innovative ideas needed to design and build our future. Restructuring our financial system to meet new demands is vital to rebuilding families. Only your support will create our bright future.

"Unlike congress, I refuse to do nothing. You did not elect me to do nothing. Bold action must be taken now. The success of our future will depend on innovation and new thinking—like the ZERO Plan. Moving from recovery to dynamic growth must be founded on the new ideas presented in the ZERO Plan. As Americans, our strength comes from our ability to work together. Together, we can do ZERO.

"Thank you! God bless you. And may God bless the United States of America!"

Day 8: World's Largest Shark Tank

It was seven a.m. on Wednesday, January 25, 2012, I was meeting with Dick Melong and Wrecking Balls to create my speaking points and press release. We had to react quickly to the fallout from the State of the Union Speech. We were in the Avalanche Ski Lodge Bar in the Scott Free Capitol Bar. I was badly in need of a Dick Melong FUC Plan. The fireplace was going as we sat at a table with oversized leather chairs. Everybody ordered and was anxious to get started.

"Look, Dick, I will not get elected if I do not come out punching on this ZERO Plan. OBaby is taking our eye off the ball with this helping consumer garbage," I said.

"I was ready for damage control on this one and already made up some notes," said Dick.

"How are you doing since being struck by lightning?" asked Wrecking Balls.

"Better. It has made me rethink my life," said Dick, smiling.

"I have heard some stories about your training seminars," said Wrecking Balls.

"I don't want to hurt our party. Let me cover my notes here, and you decide. I am not going to be introducing anything new. This is damage control," said Dick.

"Yes. Sounds good," I said.

"We have to use the Kick-In-The-Balls FUC Plan. This involves fiercely attacking opponents with lies, unlimited campaign cash to fund lies, and consistently and forcibly keeping on message. Sound OK?" asked Dick.

KICK-IN-THE-BALLS FUC PLAN

- Fiercely attack opponents with lies
- Unlimited campaign cash to fund lies
- Consistently and forcibly keeping on message

"It is doable," said Wrecking Balls.

"You can sound forcible only for so long until you just look like a grumpy old man and turn off voters," I said.

"We can use the same old lies we usually tell of cutting pretend regulations and less taxes for the rich. This ZERO Plan is just another OBaby entitlement program," said Wrecking Balls.

"Our Goldballs'n Sak Super PAC (Paid Access Corruption) can provide the unlimited cash. I think you did it again, Dick. Thanks," I said.

"You're welcome," Dick said, nodding.

"I am going to leave you to do the press release and my speaking points. I am just going to sit here by the fire and call Han Jahb about his equity meltdown." I took my phone out and sat by the fire.

Wall Street banking stocks had started to melt down around the world. The threat of OBaby ending zero interest loans, requiring minimum taxation, and of Americans withdrawing from retirement accounts would hurt short-term profits. The banks and investment houses predicted that the ZERO Plan would cause a run on investment accounts. They feared that financial institutions wouldn't be able to grow. Steptin Schibt Bank stock was tanking in premarket.

The bank had just opened its lavish headquarters, which was called the Shark Tank. The seventy-seven-story glass tower in Lower Manhattan cost $700 million, and was sometimes called the 777 Tower. It was the most opulent office tower ever built, a shrine to arrogance and power. Steptin Schibt Bank was the institution for turning investing into gambling. The tower was the center of power looming over a global interconnected financial system, which was to challenge its largest competitor—Las Vegas.

Han Jahb was sitting in his new office having a mimosa at seven thirty a.m. when I called him.

"I am sure you know our stock is tanking. This ZERO Plan needs to end," said Han.

"Well, it would be good for business in the long run," I said.

"We know I am paid hundreds of millions for short-term profits. I don't care about anything else," said Han.

"I heard you talked to Butch and Chainsaw after the speech," I said.

"Yes, I want to merge with them. This will stabilize the meltdown," said Han. "They want out. Butch admitted to being too drunk to run such a large and complex institution. Chainsaw is ready to go."

"This would be difficult to get by the Financial Services Committee Chairman," I said.

"Correct. Do you know where Harry Brokass is right now? He is vacationing in Las Vegas during this crisis. Who is this idiot?" Han said loudly.

"I am sure you have already called OBaby," I said.

"Yes, I am just waiting for him to return my call. You better get elected because this helping the consumer is destroying us," said Han.

"Thanks," I said.

"Wait. Can you tell me one thing? How did you know to sell your Steptin Schibt stock?" asked Han.

"You need to exploit political intelligence and you did say to sell your stock at the shareholder meeting also," I said.

"You got me on that one," said Han, laughing.

At 9:20 a.m., the White House called Han and connected him to President OBaby Domay.

"How are you?" asked OBaby.

"I am considering getting a Harry Brokass tailored wetsuit. I just haven't had enough to drink yet," said Han.

"That's a good one. I didn't expect that," said OBaby, smiling.

"We need your help," Han implored.

"Butch and Chainsaw told me you want to merge," said OBaby.

"Yes, this will stop the train wreck," said Han. "We also need a bailout."

OBaby said icily, "I have no idea why you are not in jail. You never paid back the zero-interest loans. How can you ask for more?"

"The idea of the ZERO Plan is destroying us," Han said. "I need a loan modification with my bailout. You allow us to do whatever we want and must pay the bailout as we expect."

"I am going to do ZERO," OBaby told him. "Nobody is going to stop me from doing ZERO. I will fight you and Super Congress World to help American families."

"This is not a time for fake leadership," Han told him.

"Really?" OBaby was angry. "You know, I heard you have a new Shark Tank. I have a question. Is the story true about how your new Shark Tank was paid for? Fixing Wall Street has been a major concern of mine. There is a joke going around that you built the Shark Tank from government welfare. You took our zero-interest loans and loaned it back to us at 2.7 percent interest. What new scam are you trying to work me over with now? Unsecured zero-interest loans were used to purchase Treasury securities that earned 2.7 percent interest. You loaned us our own money back, and we paid you interest. You collected interest on risk-free investments. Who *wins* when you can play golf at Super Congress World? Because you are not in jail, we get scammed again and again."

"I have to take credit for the new Shark Tank, and yes, we did loan you back your money for risk-free interest," Han replied. "This is not my best work. My best work was when the market tanked in 2008. We make money if the market goes up or down. We made billions on the market going down. We knew what was going to happen and shorted the market. Market manipulations and misinformation are what I do best. I also made money on the market going up the past three years. Your ZERO Plan will eliminate the progress made."

"Why don't you find some financial analysts, economists, and statisticians to say you are going to report record profits this quarter? If doing ZERO is going to destroy you, go bankrupt. Our creative economy allows you to discover solutions. Our financial system can recover without you," said OBaby.

"Your leadership caused this and requires you to fix it," shouted Han.

"Sometimes in life we make mistakes and should pay the price," OBaby snapped. "You might fail, but new businesses will take your place. They might even be ethical and not look for government handouts. They might provide real services and not just lie and scheme. Smaller and stable banks are fine. You are going to get the same loan mod as Harry Brokass. Good-bye."

OBaby slammed the phone down, then asked for Harry Brokass to be called. Harry immediately picked up when he saw the White House calling.

"You will not believe this," OBaby said. "Han Jahb wants a loan modification. This is crazy. I told him no, of course. Just because they own Super Congress World, they think they are above the law and basic human decency."

"Did you know that Steptin Schibt Bank wants to merge with BIG?" Brokass asked. "It will be called Big Schibt Bank. It will be the largest out-of-control enigma corporation in the history of the world. Too big to fail has failed, and financial institutions are becoming larger than ever."

"They will be just fine," OBaby said. "Doing whatever they want and paying the huge legal settlements means Wall Street is back. Wall Street is making billions. Business is back to normal when it's paying enormous fraud settlements."

"It would be asking too much for them to pay interest on their free government loans," Harry said. "They convinced us that paying interest is too risky, especially with the large legal settlements they need to pay on their fraudulent and deceptive business practices.

They have fooled us into believing that the slightest increase in regulations, repeal of tax breaks, incurrence of any risk, or elimination of zero-interest loans could cause our financial system to collapse."

"I have got to go," OBaby cut him off. "Enjoy Vegas!"

"Thanks. I'll talk to you soon, Mr. President," said Harry.

You can make a lot of money shorting stocks, or betting they will lose value. Something like that could make you a lot of money if you knew about the ZERO Plan before it was announced.

Harry went to Las Vegas to spend the weekend with his parents on vacation. It was ten a.m., and he was meeting them for two-for-one margaritas at his favorite breakfast buffet.

Carol Brokass, Harry's mom, loaded up her plate and sat down. "I am so glad all of us are here today. Also, the buffet has no gator. I think I am OK with that because the beer is ice cold."

"This is my favorite buffet," said Harry.

"I'm glad you got rid of your man tits," said Carol.

"Thanks," said Harry, wincing.

"Thanks for letting me know about the ZERO Plan on the State of the Union Speech," Warren Brokass said. "I have to tell you what I've done. I shorted the stock market in your account. There is now four million dollars in your account."

"Dad, you can't do that," Harry said. "Are you crazy? You gambled my retirement!"

"No, no, no. Wall Street does this as standard practice and just pays the settlement. We are keeping the money. I want more than just Social Security. We are keeping the four million. I am a signer on your account."

"You just know my passwords in case of emergency!" Harry said loudly. "I can't believe you. I can't believe we are arguing about this. You're jeopardizing everything I have worked my entire life for."

"No, you told me elected officials are exempt from insider trading," said Warren.

"It is unethical. My next project was to stop the profiting from nonpublic information. How will I do this with your betting in my account?" asked Harry.

"We all know you are exempt from the law and will not go to jail for using insider information like Wall Street," said Warren. "Congress is just as corrupt as Wall Street. You told me this was allowed."

"Yes, because this is unethical and must be changed. It is not right, even if legal. It causes politicians to just look after self-interests and not serve the public," said Harry. "Wall Street will always buy corrupt politicians, just as they corrupted you to legally steal four million dollars. They will buy whomever they want."

"Guess what? Profiting from legal stealing is *legal*," said Warren.

"No, you wait," Harry said. "I need to explain how it really works. I need to point out that the Dick Melong Wall Street Reform was itself a worthless security. The only way to beat Wall Street was at their own game. We sold them what they sold us—worthless security. You can beat Wall Street only if it is at their own game. They now need to pay the bill for worthless security and not us. We gave them everything to cause a financial bubble. Asset values needed to double in two to three years. This allows the ZERO Plan to transfer Wall Street wealth back to American families. Wall Street is being played here, not us. The ZERO Plan resets our economy back to protecting and preserving families. The ZERO Plan would not work without a financial bubble created by the Dick Melong Wall Street Reform and Rewarding Extortion Act. OBaby just played the game of the last administration—Butch and Chainsaw."

"Now, you think I'm crazy," Warren said. "But I'm keeping the four million dollars. You know I am right."

"I ended up corrupting my dad," Harry muttered. "You used insider information."

"I did not use any taxpayer money. I used your retirement savings," said Warren.

Harry said, "I just wanted to legally take back the $200,000 in my retirement accounts using the ZERO Plan. I want to just be financially free today. My retirement savings will pay off my mortgage. No more begging for a loan modification. Super Congress World is going to give me a great government pension and all of my health care costs paid for the rest of my life. My own retirement money will help me live today better."

"You don't rob a bank and not plan to get away with it on all counts," said Warren. "I enjoy day trading stock options. Wall Street operates on insider information to unfairly steal cash from my options trading. Political intelligence is all I needed to cash in."

Harry asked, " How do you think I can get away with this?"

"Nobody will think you did anything wrong because I used stock index options. No specific stocks were purchased that could imply self-interest.

Investigators will think you are a stud horse for hitting a jackpot," said Warren.

"Great, I can just put that I am a stud horse on my disclosure form, and they will understand," said Harry.

"You got it!" said Warren laughing with Carol.

"I have to explain some new legislation I am sponsoring," said Harry. "It involves Disclosing Insider Congressional Knowledge or DICK. When something involves the financial markets and our government, full disclosure is needed with DICK. Giving DICK is what works for Congress."

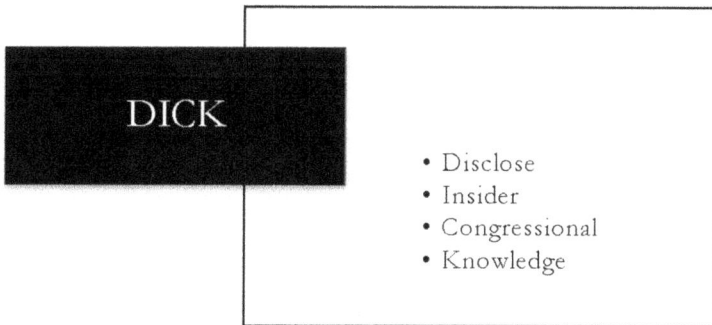

DICK

- Disclose
- Insider
- Congressional
- Knowledge

"Good luck with that," said Warren.

"No matter what, we don't have to worry about me going to jail. As an elected official, insider trading is protected in the constitution under the Speech or Debate Clause. This means I don't have to disclose issues related to the legislative process," Harry said.

"Good, I can sleep better," said Warren.

Carol handed Harry a handful of hundred-dollar bills. "Try to get over it. You got what you wanted—a loan modification and no more man tits. Cheers!" She touched glasses with Warren. "Let's go have fun! I'll get the check. We're not going to fight over it."

Harry said, "I cannot believe the both of you are OK with stealing four million dollars."

"It's about time your dad did something right," Carol said. "We had to be your Plan B. One thing is for sure. We all need to do something to save our hairy, broke ass."

Day 9: Naked Friday Golfing with Strippers on Trampolines

The journey of figuring out my life had now taken me to a therapist. It was difficult finding a therapist who would allow me to have martinis during our sessions. I made it clear that this was needed to fully understand my predicament. My therapist eventually learned how to make an excellent apple martini and had one ready for me at every appointment. Picking up the pieces and learning to deal with the truth were more than I could handle alone. The vodka also caused other side effects I had been in denial of. Therapy was the only way for me to come to terms with it.

My wife and I had redecorated all of our homes around the world. We got two Bichon Frise dogs from a pet rescue and enjoyed going antiquing with them as we purchased new things for our homes. We were getting great deals because Baby Boomers were selling many of their cherished and priceless heirlooms for food and other living expenses. She was very supportive of my alternative lifestyle. There was no way I would ever tell my friends the side effects of my vodka. It was like watching a train wreck as I got professional help.

On Friday, January 27, 2012, the most powerful game of golf occurred. It was astounding that it happened to be on Naked Friday Golfing With Strippers On Trampolines. It was eleven a.m. when my Super Congress World phone warning woke me in bed with my wife and boyfriend. I reached over to get the phone from the nightstand when my boyfriend gave me a big hug. I apologized to him and my wife after giving her a long kiss. Then I made a mimosa before going onto the terrace. When I looked back in the French doors, they were spooning because my wife does not like being alone.

OBaby, Butch, and Chainsaw were on my phone at the Steptin Schibt Capitol Golf Course. For eight years under the Butch and Chainsaw administration, I had owned them. They needed to confront President OBaby on a deal that would get done. The three of them had to meet. Have I bought President OBaby? You do not see me in jail. We will just pay the settlement because I own Super Congress World. There were rumors that OBaby wanted to meet with experts on technology, housing, or stock market bubbles. This was a job for Butch and Chainsaw. I sat watching and listening to them when they first shook hands. One thing became clear to me while watching: if I can continue to buy the president of the United States, why should I bother with an election?

I started watching on my phone when Butch said, "The fresh-cut grass and flowers smell incredible. Let's get a drink."

"I thought Harry Brokass was going to join us," said Chainsaw.

"He went to Las Vegas with his family," said OBaby.

"I guess we will have a threesome," said Chainsaw as they all sat down at the bar and ordered on the touch screen.

"I am glad you could meet with me on such short notice," said OBaby.

"That was some State of the Union Speech," said Chainsaw.

"Wall Street has been slamming me since," said OBaby. "Everybody is worried about their short-term profits when my economic vision is long-term. This will help them build their business. I was hoping for advice."

"When I was in office, Wrecking Balls did all my thinking," said Butch. "I do have to say thank you for the Dick Melong Wall Street Reform and Rewarding Extortion Act. It was brilliant!" said Butch. "We have made billions."

"This was just was the first step," OBaby said. "I now need to help individuals without destroying the progress we've made. I think I might have burst a financial bubble with the speech. Cash must now be in the hands of American families to manage, and not the crooks I play golf with. I need advice from you two bubble machines."

"Keep the focus on the consumer to mitigate any damage from your Wall Street market concerns," said Butch. "Goldballs'n Sak, with the help of Super Congress World, will attack you with lies as they always do. I know he met with Dick Melong and Wrecking Balls, who gave him some FUC Plan that involves absolute lies."

"To help mitigate the consequences of my plan, I am trying to increase home values and get home improvement and construction going again. Real estate creates millions of jobs." OBaby said. "It is the only way to add jobs, stability and solid growth to our economy. To get this done, I am going to bypass Super Congress World."

"If you're going directly to the people, certain things must be done," Butch told him. "We know how to engineer illusion. Wrecking Balls did teach me a few things. People must feel hopeful. Buying hope with borrowed money always works. If it doesn't, use fear and anger instead."

Chainsaw said, "Most importantly, confident, bold leadership is the only change that people will accept. Helping consumers with zero-interest loans is bold. If this does not work, make sure only yes men get elected to go along with lies and forget the people."

"You know, the fear thing is not me," OBaby said. "Unprecedented access to capital will ignite our economy again like my ZERO Plan. Bringing back consumer demand is the only way for businesses to start hiring again."

Chainsaw said, "Not destroying Wall Street's latest bubble will be tricky. You will need solid economic growth to expand the economy. Free money has caused the stock market to double in three years. Free money has no risk. With no risk, businesses become reckless and destructive. They make us think that if you raise interest rates or change the tax code, the bubble will burst. You are in a very precarious situation, Mr. President."

"They are still supported by corporate welfare," Butch said. "Be extremely careful to not play the Super Congress World game of stealing paychecks."

"Just make the American public feel something real and meaningful," Chainsaw said. "Get the people to believe we're on the right track. Exploit the universal need to feel hopeful. Remember, if that doesn't work, use fear."

"It will be tricky to get Super Congress World and Wall Street to allow Americans to receive help," OBaby said. "Even if a financial bubble bursts, should we care about Wall Street ever again after what had to be done to stabilize the global financial system?"

"I'll drink to that," Butch said.

"Time to start," said Chainsaw walking to the tee.

"I'm going to leave my boxers on," OBaby said. "You guys can do your thing."

"I have seen your naked ass out here before. Something must be wrong," said Butch.

"It is surprising me that you have not heard any rumors. I like to watch football naked on Sundays. I was having nachos with hot cheese. It was real hot when I spilled it on my junk. Greasy cheese stuck to me when I got up to yell at the TV. I screamed so loud that everybody in the White House came to the TV room and saw my junk!" said OBaby, laughing.

"You dumb ass," said Butch.

"I am still in recovery mode," said OBaby, gaining his composure.

"If it makes you feel better, my drunk ass has been seen peeing off the Truman Balcony many times," said Butch.

"I love not having to worry about sunburn down here, because that would really hurt," said Chainsaw.

"Now wait, your spray tan is bright orange, and I can't believe you didn't get nude for it. Your junk is white," Butch said.

"Do I look too orange? I am trying to look less like the living dead," Chainsaw said.

"If you don't look like the living dead, people will think there is something wrong," Butch said.

"That's bright orange with a white ass," OBaby said, smiling.

"OK, I am leaving my jock strap on," Butch said. "I don't want to strain my package like the last time I was out here."

"Where do you get a red jock strap?" OBaby asked, chuckling. "That is too sexy for golfing. All you need are red wings."

"I *had* red wings, but with my blackout drinking, I have no idea what happened to them," Butch said, and shrugged. "This is tailored from the Birds of Prey Bipartisan Gift Shop. Look how nice this fits my ass and shows off my package. It looks a lot bigger with the tailoring."

"Nice," said OBaby.

"Now, I just got my cast off my ribs, so I need to take this slow," said Butch.

"How did you injure your ribs, anyway?" asked OBaby.

"This is embarrassing," Butch said. "I was having some, uh, fun on the stripper pole in the bathhouse steam room. I was swinging away with my legs in the air when I moved my hand onto the wet pole. I was moving fast when I shot off and pounded a really hot guy who broke my fall. Two lower ribs got fractured, but it could have been worse. I'm considering leaving my wife because I enjoyed it so much."

"Well at least the story has a happy ending," Chainsaw said.

"It's just friends with benefits—nothing too serious that my wife needs to know," said Butch.

"Right, how many times have I heard that?" Chainsaw asked.

"Wow! Look at that. Can you really do that on a trampoline?" Butch said.

"Beautiful!" Chainsaw said. "I wish my wife could see that. It would hurt her back, but the other woman could help."

"Your wife had no problem doing it with me!" Butch said. "Just kidding! Just kidding!"

Getting back to business, OBaby said, "I need your advice about dealing with Super Congress World."

"You need Dick to get anything through Super Congress World," said Butch.

"Dick needs to be kept out of this because I am trying to help only the people," OBaby said. "Wall Street and big business are already addicted to corporate welfare and tax benefits."

"How do you expect to get anything through Super Congress World without Dick?" asked Chainsaw.

"Look, I don't need Dick. You might need Dick or Han Jahb to get things done, but I need to go directly to the people to get this done," said OBaby.

"Have you heard that Dick and Han Jahb have something going on?" said Chainsaw, laughing. "That reminds me of a great joke. Dick and Han are going to get married. They are calling it the 'Dick Marries Hand Wedding.' I love it!"

"Let's have another round. I could use an apple martini," Butch said, and they ordered on the touch screen golf cart. "I don't understand why people think that nothing gets done around here. My office desk is hurting my back. It was so bad that I went for a massage, and now I am having trouble walking. Have you ever tried the Spread Eagle Massage?"

"Yes, and I was OK after the physical therapy," Chainsaw said. "Yesterday, I went for the Eagle Catches the Squirrel Massage. The swelling finally went down this morning. I thought I wasn't going to make it out here, especially with all the snow and ice on the roads from my hotel."

"Wait, is that Dick Melong and Han Jahb playing golf on the other course in the far distance?" asked Butch.

"Yes, I see them. Dick is only wearing his usual nylons and thong underwear," said OBaby.

"I have to say that Dick does have a big putter," said Chainsaw as Dick teed off. "That underwear must really ride up his butt when he swings."

"He has a nice stroke, but he needs to spread his legs more," said Butch. "Since we are talking about Wall Street, does anybody know what SHAFT Trading is?"

"It's the same thing that caused you to hurt your ribs," said Chainsaw, laughing.

"It is trading technique that lasts less than a second and is completely unregulated because we are not supposed to understand it," OBaby said.

"Han Jahb was telling me about it, so it must be a scam," Butch told him. " He must really think we believe the things he says. It does sound like the ultimate way to legally steal retirement, though."

"He does own Super Congress World," OBaby said. "I am tired of his ass kissing and looking for special tax treatment to pay for Super Congress World."

"We're hearing that you want to make changes to the tax code," Butch said. "And I am all for ass kissing to not pay taxes. Let's have another round."

"Our company helps pay for all of this, so favorable tax treatment is good business and not ass kissing," Chainsaw said. "Not that there is anything wrong with ass kissing when you look at how Super Congress World operates. Maybe Dick Melong should do a seminar on how to effectively to kiss ass."

"I have a gift for you. I recently adopted two Italian Greyhounds from a pet rescue. One of them was humping a stuffed animal in my living room when I came home last weekend. I have no idea how he found it. I had it cleaned and re-stuffed to return to you," said Butch as he took a store bag from his golf bag and gave it to OBaby.

OBaby opened it, and it was his blue unicorn. "I knew you had stolen it. It is not as if I could go around asking for it back. Thanks. Do you know the story behind this?"

"Only rumors," said Butch.

"This is from two Swedish cheerleaders I met in my sexual addiction program when I was in college," said OBaby.

"That's exactly what I heard," said Chainsaw.

"No, it is not what you think. They are male cheerleaders. I got them a job here at Super Congress World when I came into office," said OBaby.

"Butch knows them, I am sure," said Chainsaw, laughing.

"OK, lets change topics," said Butch. "This is a great time to bring up our merger. You know we want to merge with Steptin Schibt Bank, so they would be more powerful than ever."

"Let me talk this over with my magical blue unicorn here," said OBaby, laughing.

Chainsaw said, "Bad Insurance Group merging with Steptin Schibt Bank—Big Schibt. It will be even more impossible to regulate or tax our business. This will create the largest company in the world. We have to have your support."

"'You want me to support Big Schibt Bank? 'Too big to fail' has been a failure anyway," OBaby said. "Financial institutions are larger than ever, while living off of zero-interest loans and getting favorable tax treatment."

"You want to help American families, but we are the gatekeeper for that help," Chainsaw told the president. "Super Congress World needs the complete control that Butch and I can provide."

"I understand your point, but it's risky having another large corporation that nobody can understand as you suck up this nation's wealth. Falling into the abyss of an enigmatic corporation will create a point of no return. Business and political leaders cannot handle the convoluted complexities of an enormous Big Schibt enigma that will create a financial black hole. Now you want Big Schibt to have full control over Super Congress World. This puts us on the brink of a final breaking point."

"Corporations need complete control of our government. Voters need to step in line. If you get in our way on this, I will support Goldballs'n Sak for president. We will get what we want," said Chainsaw.

"You think I cannot fight you. Don't you?" said OBaby, smiling. "I am just a speed bump to getting what you want.

"We know how to get things done," said Butch.

"You will still need to get this approved by the Financial Services Committee. With Harry Brokass a chairman, your merger will not go through," said OBaby, smirking.

"Harry will fall in line. We will convince him that the deal will make him millions. Let's remember, it is Super Congress World that makes stealing legal," said Butch.

"Look where Harry is now. He is in Las Vegas hoping to get 777 on a slot machine for a jackpot. He is ours," said Chainsaw.

"I love Las Vegas, too. I am over Wall Street," said OBaby.

"There is one thing I don't understand about Harry Brokass," said Butch. "What's with the tattoos?"

"I agree," Chainsaw said. "He is maybe ten years younger than we are."

"It's probably a midlife crisis," Butch said. "Do you need to be sober to experience something like that? Let's all go get tattoos when we're done playing. I'm buying!" "Maybe," said OBaby as Chainsaw just glared at Butch.

"I understand your concerns," Butch said. "Helping American families will require leadership that needs us to be the means to an end. We buy the sellout politicians you need to get your agenda through."

"A huge company like Big Schibt will create a financial black hole that will destroy all of us," OBaby said. "We have to work together to survive. A decade has been lost because we didn't realize this reality. It is one thing to wreck your own life, and it is another to wreck a country! Maybe Americans don't realize their democracy is on the brink of destruction because their house is being foreclosed on or their child is crying. This town has sold out our democracy. The people will take back their CAPITAOL—one vote at a time.

www.ingramcontent.com/pod-product-compliance
Lightning Source LLC
Chambersburg PA
CBHW050126280326
41933CB00010B/1271